THE UNITED NATIONS
IN A NEW WORLD ORDER

The Keck Center for International and Strategic Studies is a non-partisan and non-profit research organization, founded at Claremont McKenna College in 1983 with an endowment grant from the W. M. Keck Foundation. The Keck Center fosters education and research about the critical aspects of contemporary international affairs and strategic issues. It sponsors lecture series, student fellowships, visiting scholars, conferences, and publications. The Keck Center's programs are supported by gifts and endowments from individuals, corporations, and foundations, and by the sale of publications and conference fees.

CLAREMONT McKENNA COLLEGE

THE UNITED NATIONS
IN A NEW WORLD ORDER

Edwin M. Smith

Michael G. Schechter

The Keck Center for International and Strategic Studies

Monograph Series, Number Six

Library of Congress Cataloging-in-Publication Data

The united nations in a new world order / Edwin M. Smith, Michael G. Schechter.
    p.   cm. -- (Monograph series / The Keck Center for International and Strategic Studies ; no. 6)
    Includes bibliographical references.
    Contents: Collective security and collective defense / Edwin M. Smith -- The United Nations in the aftermath of Somalia / Michael G. Schechter.
    ISBN: 0-930607-17-1
    1. United Nations.   2. Security, International.
3. International agencies.   I. Smith, Edwin M.   Collective security and collective defense. 1994.   II. Schechter, Michael G.   United Nations in the aftermath of Somalia.   1994.
III. Series: Monograph series (Keck Center for International and Strategic Studies) ; no. 6.

JX1977.U42595   1994
341.7'2--dc20   93-50867
                                                                      CIP

The Keck Center for International and Strategic Studies
Claremont McKenna College
850 North Columbia Avenue
Claremont, California   91711-6420
(909) 621-8213

Manufactured in the United States of America

Table of Contents

Acknowledgment

The Keck Center is pleased to issue the two papers written by Edwin M. Smith and Michael G. Schechter, respectively, as its monograph. The papers which were originally presented at a conference held in the spring of 1993, under the Keck Center's auspices, are subsequently revised and published without much editorial change.

I wish to thank Michael Cernea (The World Bank), Denise Dresser (Mexican Autonomous Technical Institute), Thomas Ilgen (Pitzer College), Robert Loftis (Department of State), Nüket Kardam (Monterey Institute of International Studies), Harold W. Rood (Claremont McKenna College), and Carol Wise (Claremont Graduate School) for their participation in the conference, Dante Corricello and Jennifer Serventi for their service as student rapporteurs, and Mary Anderson for her administrative assistance.

Chae-Jin Lee
Director

January 1994

Collective Security and Collective Defense: Changing Conceptions and Institutions

Edwin M. Smith[*]

Introduction

The end of the Cold War has altered circumstances that have been regarded for forty years as the immutable cornerstones of international relations.[1] These changes have generated challenges to hallowed norms and to the institutions that have embodied them. Organizations established after World War II, designed to respond to certain anticipated threats, have been less than satisfactory vehicles for collective reaction to new and unanticipated threats. Meanwhile, norms that once limited international concern for problems within states no longer preclude multilateral action to remedy humanitarian emergencies. As changing arrangements have forced adjustments by international institutions, government actors now recognize the serious limitations that infect the principles that have ordered their relationships.

Many questions have been raised as new international players have initiated actions that defy traditional norms, facing diplomats and government leaders with unimagined challenges. Conventional notions of political and territorial integrity have been rocked as self-determination and secessionist movements have shattered the stability of many states. At the same time, evolving crises have forced multilateral organizations into actions which implicitly challenge settled doctrines about the scope of the domestic jurisdiction of states.

[*]Professor of Law and International Relations, University of Southern California. This article expands upon an earlier chapter in W. Andy Knight and Keith Krause, eds., *United Nations Reform for the Twenty-First Century* (forthcoming).

This "new world order" forces us to rethink conceptual structures that have become comfortable lenses for our view of world politics. We may be confronting the frustrations involved in attempting to analyze and generalize from our limited understandings of contingent and evolving events.[2] While rethinking may force us into drastically new and different visions, the results may prove to be rewarding.

The current apparent global disorder may simply reflect the inadequacies of our implicit assumptions as observers.[3] Similarly, the seeming ineptitude of existing international institutions may also show the frailty of their foundational conceptions. We may be involved in an effort to understand an opaque reality where anachronistic institutions rely too comfortably on traditional norms as they attempt to address vaguely comprehensible conflicts. If we have concerns about the limitations and possibilities of international institutions, we need to reconsider both sets of assumptions.

Questions of international peace and security dominate many discussions of international relations. Those questions become far more complex in the changed global realities. While some of dangers that plagued several generations of Cold War diplomats remain important, surprising new dangers have managed to arise, forcing reconsideration of postwar security institutions. Other problems, initially omitted from the taxonomy of international security threats, have come to be seen as demanding urgent action. In this new and changing context, traditional institutional structures have endured tremendous stresses; whether they can cope with unconventional threats remains to be seen.

Two principal approaches have been adopted for responding to threats to international peace and security. One of them, collective security, involves a commitment of all states to respond to the aggression of any refractory state or group of states. The United Nations provides the primary example of an institutional structure founded on collective security. The second approach, collective defense, establishes a commitment by members of a limited alliance to act in mutual self-defense. The North Atlantic Treaty Organization (NATO) stands as the exemplar of collective defense institutions.

This essay will begin by considering these two traditional approaches to international peace and security, looking at the founding assumptions and the organizational structures of the two institutions that best embody those approaches. It will then briefly examine the performance of those institutions in the Cold War context. Next, it will survey some of the new threats to international peace and security that appear likely to arise; alternative conceptual approaches will be explored, providing indications of the limitations of analyses and prescriptions based upon traditional assumptions of state power and interest. Most importantly, the essay will consider the prospects for collective defense and collective security institutions to respond adequately to the new world disorder. The essay will conclude by briefly considering the prospects for cooperative interaction between these institutions as a means to remedy their respective limitations in coping with new and different threats to global security.[4]

Two Approaches to Peace

We can begin our analysis of the limits of the foundational assumptions with an analysis of collective security and collective defense. These two ideas have similarities in their reliance on collective modalities of response. Because of these similarities, the terms are sometimes used interchangeably. At bottom, however, they do distinguish between two different approaches to the problems of peace and war, each of which addresses massive international violence as the principal question. They have been incorporated into two different institutional structures in the United Nations and NATO.

Collective Security

The first, collective security, requires universal participation in a system of multilateral responses to any potential threat to any individual state. Collective security adopts a universalistic theory. Under that approach, the solution to international violence requires the commitment of the entire world community to a system in which all states agree to take common action to end the threat to peace.[5] Collective security assumes that peace and security are indivisible; every member of the international community must respond by sanctioning the actions of any actor that breaches or threatens to breach the peace.

The United Charter[6] codifies the most widely accepted conception of universal collective security.[7] As a universal organization, the United Nations adopted specific institutional rules and generally applicable norms for the preservation of international peace and security. The rules, found in Article 2(4) and Chapter VII of the Charter, embody norms adapted from League of Nations institution by the victorious allies of World War II.[8] The Charter norms reject the application of actual or potential military force for purposes of territorial acquisition or political coercion. Charter rules establish a system of enforcement obligating member states to support collective actions adjudged to be necessary by the Security Council. Many scholars and practitioners of the United Nations system refer to this collection of norms and rules as the international collective security system.

Collective Defense

The second approach to multilateral response to threats, collective defense, has been described as "selective security."[9] That approach depends on the formation of alliances by limited numbers of states against commonly recognized threats. Members of the alliance agree to come to the assistance of any member if an outside actor attacks. Conflicts that do not involve the members of the alliance do not necessarily merit any collective alliance response; in fact, alliance members adopt individual policies for reacting to these outside eventualities. Only when one of the members of the alliance is threatened or assaulted will alliance members respond collectively.

The North Atlantic Treaty created the most successful contemporary example of a collective defense alliance.[10] That agreement established legal obligations and political relationships among the signatory states that committed each of them to treat an attack on any party by a non-party as an attack on all members. As a result, the NATO Treaty alliance protects those formally obligated by the treaty; it is a particularist rather than a universalist security arrangement. In addition, the treaty imposes no generally applicable norms that bind nonmembers to refrain from the use of force.[11]

Collective security and collective defense rely upon different consensus assumptions and different obligations to accomplish protection against threats to international peace and security. In the past, the success of these two strategies has been mixed. As the conditions of the international order change with the end of the Cold War, so do the sources of threats. The primary purpose of this essay is to evaluate the potential for either collective defense or collective security institutions to provide constructive responses to new international threats, and to suggest possible benefits to be gained from coordination between those different types of institutions.

The United Nations and Collective Security

The institutional structure of the U.N. is based upon the formal obligations created by the United Nations Charter. The Charter, adopted in San Francisco in 1945, provides the most widely accepted statement of the formal international codes of behavior applicable to the use of force and violence. The most basic norm, found in Article 2(4), is simply stated:

> All Members shall refrain in their international relations from the threat or use of force against the territorial integrity or political independence of any state, or in any other manner inconsistent with the Purposes of the United Nations.

The Charter includes a potentially limiting principle in Article 2(7) which says that "[n]othing contained in the present Charter shall authorize the United Nations to intervene in matters essentially within the domestic jurisdiction of any state. . . ." Article 24 of the Charter confers upon the Security Council primary responsibility for the maintenance of international peace and security, granting primary responsibility to the five permanent members who participated in the coalition that emerged victorious from World War II. Article 25 obligates the member states to carry out the decisions of the Council.

Chapter VII of the United Nations Charter describes the norms and mechanisms of collective enforcement. The articles of that Chapter outline the procedures for Security Council response to international violence. Article 39 authorizes the Council to "determine the existence of any threat to the peace, breach of the peace, or act of aggression. . . ." Once the

Council has exercised its Art. 39 authority to determine that such a threat exists, the Council may call upon the involved states under Art. 40 to comply with those provisional measures necessary to terminate the threat. The Security Council response to the Iraqi invasion of Kuwait provides a recent example of this determination. In passing Resolution 660, the Council, having determined that "there exists a breach of international peace and security" and "[a]cting under Articles 39 and 40 of the Charter", "[c]ondemns the Iraqi invasion" and "[d]emands that Iraq withdraw immediately and unconditionally. . . ."[12]

Article 41 of the Charter provides that the Security Council "may decide what measures not involving the use of armed force are to be employed to give effect to its decisions" and may call upon the members to give effect to those measures. Again, the Iraq crisis provides a clear example. When the occupation of Kuwait continued, the Council imposed mandatory economic sanctions. Resolution 661 called upon all states to adopt import, export and financial sanctions against Iraq. The same resolution established the Sanctions Committee to undertake supervision of implementation and enforcement.

Under Article 42, the Charter provides the authorization for the resort to collective force to terminate breaches of international peace. Returning to the Gulf example, Operation Desert Storm did not fall precisely within the framework of Article 42, which would have required the command of the relevant forces to function through the Security Council.

The institutional structure that grew from the Charter's formalities has evolved through periods of turmoil and stagnation. At first, excessive optimism accompanied the founding of the United Nations.[13] However, evidence of difficulties began to mount quickly as crises developed in Azerbaijan, the Middle East, Berlin, and Korea.[14] By the end of the latter conflict, the Cold War cast a pall over all of the initiatives considered by the institution.

The Cold War saw the frustration of many of the early expectations of those who developed the collective security concept. One of the primary problems resulted from the use of the veto by both the U.S. and the Soviet Union, each seeking to prevent Security Council action advocated by the other. Repetition of this sort of manipulation cast a shadow upon the credibility of the Security Council.[15] At one point, a noted British military analyst wrote that the United Nations:

> has failed in its primary task. It has not created a new world order in which every state derives its security from the collective strengths of the whole. It reflects the disorders, fears and rivalries of the world as it is, and does what it can to mitigate them.[16]

This failure was attributed in substantial part to "dissention among its leading members."[17] That dissention had paralyzed attempts by the UN to implement measures of collective security. Those measures could be disregarded by either of the superpowers or by any state enjoying the strong support of either of them.[18] Ideological conflict between the superpowers had paralyzed institutional mechanisms for responding to threats to international peace and security.[19]

Officials in the United States based many serious criticisms of the U.N. on this and other institutional failures.[20] One official criticized United nations conventions and resolutions on terrorism and self-determination, arguing that they "do not suggest principled limits on the use of force, or any reasoned, fair-minded approach to the determination of which peoples are entitled to wage wars of national liberation."[21] Another former official found the U.N. promoting values antithetical to U.S. interests.[22] Senator Daniel Patrick Moynihan, a former U.N. Ambassador, once characterized the United Nations system as "working against moral seriousness."[23]

In the aftermath of the Gulf War, the contrast between these critical descriptions of the U.N. and more recent comments by American officials could not be more stark. Cold War animosity gave way to testaments to a new spirit of cooperation. American and Soviet leaders reached far more optimistic views of the organization.[24] In fact, the statements of the leaders of the superpowers during the Gulf conflict demonstrated astonishingly rapid changes in a global landscape thought subject only to glacial shifts.

President Bush told a joint session of Congress that the international community is moving toward "a new world order" that is "freer from the threat of terror, stronger in the pursuit of justice, and more secure in the quest for peace."[25] He highlighted the importance of collective security when he declared that "no longer can a dictator count on East-West confrontation to stymie concerted U.N. action against aggression." The President stated that "[a] new partnership of nations has begun."

Secretary of State Baker testified that the United States faced "a critical juncture in history" which is generating "one of the defining moments of . . . a new era full of promise but also one replete with new challenges."[26] Baker stated that

> the current crisis is the first opportunity . . . to reinforce the standards for civilized behavior found in the United Nations Charter and to help shape a more peaceful international order built on the promise of recent trends in Europe and elsewhere.[27]

Baker said that "it is our view . . . that we must seize the opportunity to solidify the ground rules of the new order."[28]

Agreement on very controversial United Nations actions between American and Soviet leaders gave credence to these assertions about a new order. In the Joint Statement following the Helsinki Summit, Presidents Bush and Gorbachev determined to "reaffirm . . . our support of United Nations Security Council Resolutions" and to "call upon the entire world to adhere to the sanctions mandated by the United Nations, and we pledge to work, individually and in concert to insure full compliance with the sanctions." They insisted that

> we are determined to see the present aggression end, and if the current steps fail to end it, we are prepared to consider additional ones consistent with the U.N. Charter. We must demonstrate beyond any doubt that aggression cannot and will not pay.[29]

Baker's Soviet counterpart, Foreign Minister Eduard Shevardnadze, described the Iraq crisis as posing a threat to "the emerging new world order." Speaking of the role of the United Nations, Shevardnadze reiterated the central importance of U.N. mechanisms.

> We are again becoming the United Nations and we're returning to our own global constitution; the United Nations Charter, and to those of its provisions that

were forgotten for a while but have been proven to be indispensable for the most important and vitally necessary of our tasks; the maintenance of international peace and security.[30]

The success of the coalition of states that ousted Iraq from Kuwait led to another period of voluble optimism about the prospects of the United Nations. Many commentators contended that the United Nations could now finally live up to the expectations of its founders. However, as in the early days of the U.N., new crises in surprising places stilled the celebrations.

In the wake of Desert Storm, the Security Council held its first heads-of-state summit. In the joint statement that closed the summit the heads of state noted that:

> The international community . . . faces new challenges in the search for peace. All member states expect the United Nations to play a central role at this crucial stage. The members of the Council stress the importance of strengthening and improving the United Nations to increase its effectiveness. They are determined to assume fully their responsibilities with the United Nations Organization in the framework of the Charter.

> The absence of war and military conflicts amongst states does not in itself insure international peace and security. The non-military sources of instability in the economic, social, humanitarian and ecological fields have become threats to peace and security. The United Nations membership as a whole needs to give the highest priority to the solution of these matters.[31]

This summit statement came as new collective actions demonstrated the broader visions suggested by the Council. In the past, the Security Council has been constrained from addressing many issues by contentions that action would intervene in the domestic jurisdiction of member states.[32] However, since the Gulf War, the Council has treated several internal conflicts as within its jurisdiction. The Council specifically designated Iraqi repression of the Kurds as the source of refugee flows that "threaten international peace and security."[33] Both the Cambodian and Yugoslavian peacekeeping missions have attempted to remedy internal ethnic or political conflicts. The Somali relief mission responds to humanitarian problems created by internal clan rivalry. In each instance, the activities undertaken by the United Nations have moved beyond traditional notions of threats to international peace and security. In his report, *Agenda for Peace*, Secretary Boutros Boutros-Ghali addresses a number of approaches to the broad range of new problems facing the United Nations.[34]

Before considering the problems facing the U.N. in an international system shifting away from the worship of absolute sovereignty, it is appropriate to consider the other institutional approach to international security. Defensive pacts of limited membership have served as an alternative to universal systems. The victors of World War II formed one of the world's most successful alliances in NATO.

NATO and Collective Defense

During the years immediately following World War II, the democratic European victors, confronting the broad ideological chasm that separated them from advocates of communism, adopted a different strategy to preserve security. They created an alliance that required all members to respond to external attacks on any member. In normative terms, the members of the alliance recognized the obligation to come to each other's aid when faced with attack from nondemocratic aggressors. The explicit rules of the alliance required members to treat an attack against one as an attack against all. The North Atlantic Treaty Organization (NATO) alliance expressly limited its protective cloak to benefit only its members. Commentators have characterized NATO as a collective defense alliance.

Compared to the United Nations, NATO has had more stable institutional history. While the alliance has had a number of internal crises,[35] the common values and objectives of members of the alliance allowed consensus to be reconstructed each time that it wavered. No enduring internal conflicts served to prevent the institution from fulfilling its principal purpose: providing for the collective defense of the Western democracies.

The collapse of the Warsaw Pact's Soviet-led military alliance has both blessed and cursed NATO. The demise of the eastern bloc has removed the most significant threat faced by NATO, the very reason for formation of the western alliance. At the same time, the disappearance of that threat has raised questions about the capacity of the NATO's institutional structure to responding to new threats to European peace and security. Perhaps the most telling uncertainties have been raised by current conflicts in the former Yugoslavia.

In order to appreciate the nature of the challenge that the Yugoslav conflict brings to the NATO concept of collective defense, we need to look at the institution and the values that it has adopted. We may gain a better appreciation of the limits and possibilities involved in adapting an anachronistic institution.

Scholars in international relations have used regime theory to examine institutional arrangements, focusing on the sets of principles, norms, rules, and decision-making procedures around which the expectations of particular groupings of state actors converge.[36] Participation in a regime is not general; it is limited to specific groupings of actors involved in common interest areas. In this respect, the collective security institutions established through the United Nations do not fit within the conventional usage of the concept. NATO, on the other hand, fits the theory reasonably well. This particularist-universalist distinction provides a primary difference between the concepts of collective security and collective defense.

The principles of the NATO collective defense regime reflect shared assumptions about international reality, including the tendency for totalitarian states to behave aggressively against democratic states, the inability of Western European states to confront a Soviet military threat, and the necessity for U.S. military deterrence to prevent the aggressive behavior of the Soviet Union.[37] The perception of an existing Soviet threat generated the central impetus for the formation of the western alliance.[38]

The individual members of the collective defense alliance have committed themselves to defend other members against aggression; that commitment provides the central norm of NATO, described as the "heart" of the North Atlantic Treaty.[39] The members of the European alliance undertook a specific obligation:

> The Parties agree that an armed attack against one or more of them in Europe or North America shall be considered an attack against all of them; and consequently, the agree that, it such an attack occurs, each of them . . . will assist the Party or Parties so attacked by taking forthwith, individually and in concert with other Parties, such actions as it deems necessary, including the use of armed force, to restore and maintain the security of the North Atlantic area.[40]

Article 6 of the treaty indicates that the an "armed attack on one or more of the parties" includes an armed attack "on the territory of any of the Parties in Europe or North America . . . or on the islands under the jurisdiction of any of the Parties in the North Atlantic area north of the Tropic of Cancer." The commitment also extends to "the forces, vessels, or aircraft of any of the parties, when in or over these territories . . . or the Mediterranean Sea or the North Atlantic area north of the Tropic of Cancer."

Under the western security regime, formal treaty terms established some of the rules delineating the specific mutual obligations for the states involved. For example, the central NATO commitment was to be implemented by all members "in accordance with their respective constitutional processes."[41] Other rules, though not formally expressed as treaty obligations, evolved through years of negotiation and practical routine. Decision procedures have involved an extensive and permanent bureaucracy, including the NATO Council and its Defense Committee supported by the Military Committee and the three Allied Military Commands.[42]

In many respects, NATO institutionalized the common world-views and values of the European and North American democracies on the threats posted by communism and Soviet military power enabled the construction of detailed organizational arrangements based on shared norms. So long as those common values fit with perceptions of the international order, NATO proved viable and effective. Unfortunately for NATO, perceptions and relations have changed.

The changes of the post-Cold War era have generated tremendous pressures for both collective security and collective defense institutions. As a result of these pressures, unexamined assumptions upon which the institutions were built can now be seen as offering imperfect foundations for future efforts to cope with new conflicts. At this point, we can begin to examine the strains placed upon collective security and collective defense institutions by the breakdown of the bipolar order.

Post-Cold War Institutional Stresses

New concerns have been raised about both the legitimacy of the Security Council and the effectiveness of NATO. Those concerns reflect implicit questions that go deeper than skepticism about the makeup of the Security Council or suspicion about the motives of a lonely superpower. Fresh questions arise partly in response to a "lack of fit" between these institutions and contemporary problems, reflecting an implicit challenge to the paradigm that undergirds both collective security and collective defense.

For nearly all of the postwar era, both collective security and collective defense focused on the preservation of the integrity of state actors. During the Cold War period, a comparatively stable structure characterized relationships between many states. Violent external threats to states were most often assumed to provide the most serious dangers to peace. Both the universalist and alliance-based notions shared a state-centric focus. While their institutional and organizational approaches differed, they endorsed many of the same principles.

The stable postwar order cracked with the dissolution of the eastern communist alliance and the disappearance of the Soviet Union. This reliable system served to mask serious conflicts that failed to fit within the comfortable state-centric paradigm. In many respects, the Gulf War maintained an illusion of vitality for state-centric notions of collective response. The mechanisms of the United Nations and the norms and rules of the Charter provided the framework for action against Iraq. However, the plight of Iraqi Kurds has combined with conflict in Yugoslavia and Somalia to cause serious observers to question the relevance of both conceptions of collective security. Within recent months, the most disturbing disorders have grown from conflicts within single states.

The unprecedented challenges posed by the "new international order" require both new norms and more effective means for implementing appropriate policies. International institutions devoted to the protection of traditional states become paralyzed in the face of massive disorder within states. On the other hand, collective involvement in massive internal disorders may exacerbate the fears of weaker developing states that a rebirth of neocolonialist domination may be in the offing.[43] Effective collective action will require the balancing of legitimate concern for threatened populations with respect for the political independence of those populations. It will also require a far broader range of problem-solving capabilities and areas of technical expertise than can be found in existing international security arrangements.

In order to consider the prospects for both NATO and the United Nations, some estimate must be made of the classes of future problems likely to be faced by these international institutions. Any speculations of this sort can be criticized on many grounds; almost every reasonable guess will be both correct and incorrect. These speculations must be recognized as necessary elements for any planning process; organizations must prepare for the stresses likely to be faced if they are to fulfill any significant purpose. In that light, speculation about prospective problems is unavoidable.

Dangers on the Horizon

The dangers confronting the international system can be divided into two classes for purposes of this analysis: immediate threats and instabilities that will generate tomorrow's crises, and longer term problems that pose more enduring dangers. Among the most likely immediate threats and instabilities are: nuclear proliferation; intrastate ethnic, religious, and political conflict; refugee flows and economic migrations; and interstate trade and economic conflicts. Some of these symptomatic disturbances will be magnified by longer term and more intractable dangers arise from: population expansion; global environmental degradation; and interstate conflicts arising from relative resource scarcity. The ability of international institutions to adapt to these risks and to provide remedies for the dangers realized will provide the ultimate measure of long-term viability.

The concerns about nuclear proliferation have increased dramatically with the revelation of the relative progress of the Iraqi nuclear weapons program:

> The major lesson of Iraq for the nonproliferation community is that states with a limited industrial and technological base can obtain sufficient access to bomb-making technologies and know-how to initiate a large-scale nuclear weapons program and can largely conceal that program both from national technical means of gathering intelligence and the International Atomic Energy Agency (IAEA) safeguards regime.[44]

There is greater recognition of the possibility that states party to the Non-Proliferation Treaty may conduct secret programs undiscovered by IAEA inspections.[45] Beyond this, systems of national and international technology control have proven particularly weak, leading to criticism and new legislation in some states.[46] Finally, while the end of the Cold War may have reduced certain incentives to cast a blind eye on infractions of the nonproliferation regime, trade and economic interests may provide new motivations to assist potential proliferators.[47]

Internal ethnic, religious, and political conflicts appear to many to provide a primary source of the danger of military conflict over the near future.[48] "The world's now dizzying array of ethnic hot spots . . . starkly illustrates how, of all the features of the post-Cold War world, the most consistently troubling are turning out to be the tribal hatreds that divide humankind by race, faith and nationality."[49] The most familiar case involves the former Yugoslavia, but many other conflicts have become significant in the post-Cold War environment. One recent article lists fifty-two contemporary conflicts involving ethnic, religious, or other forms of civil strife.[50]

Refugee flows arise from internal conflicts within adjacent states, political situations leading to oppression or physical insecurity, and interstate wars. These flows have caused substantial stress in neighboring states that must provide for the welfare of hundreds of thousands of indigents. Economic migrations occur as poverty-stricken populations come to believe that greater employment opportunities lie in neighboring states. The hostile reaction of the citizens of Western European states to migrants from central Europe and the Middle East has raised the specter of fascism while generating serious concern among the governments of the migrants' states of nationality.

The diplomats who structured the United Nations and the Breton Woods organizations knew full well the dangerous potential of international trade conflicts; many attributed World War II to the collapse of the global system into nationalist trade conflict.[51] While those institutions generated a significant period of prosperity, the postwar trading system faces significant pressures. Many observers see nationalist and protectionist pressures jeopardizing the continued viability of free world trade.[52] While some would argue that the substantial economic interdependence makes violent conflict over trade issues unlikely, such disagreements could certainly impair otherwise cooperative interstate relations, making peaceful dispute resolution more problematic in other arenas.

The longer term problems of population expansion, environmental degradation, and resource scarcity will probably generate some of the same symptomatic disturbances if effective responsive measures are not adopted. Refugee flows and economic migration are foreseeable results of population expansion and certain types of environmental degradation. In addition to these problems, resource scarcity could lead to embargoes as well as severe political and even military conflict.[53]

Existing institutions have been less than successful in coping with the contemporary crises posed by these immediate problems. In order to invoke the rules and procedures of international organizations, diplomats have attempted to characterize these conflicts as threats to these state-centric notions of peace and security. As a necessary condition for pursuing collective responses through traditional institutions, crises involving internal violence have been required to provide a threat to international peace and security. Internal violence remains horrendous regardless of the existence of a credible threat to neighboring states. Even when the instrumental goals of these recharacterizations are realized, both collective defense and collective security institutions based in the state-centric model have not proved adequate to respond to these bloody conflicts. States which would face few political difficulties in resisting cross-border invasions cannot easily justify risky and burdensome undertakings to end distant internal conflicts. Collective security institutions and organizations, whether universalist or alliance-based, lack norms and rules for involvement in intrastate crises, even though the loss of life may approach genocidal dimensions. These inadequacies cause critical observers to questions the utility of existing collective security institutions and organizations and the norms and rules upon which they base their actions.

If international institutions are to deal with these new problems, they must bring a broad spectrum of expertise to bear. The institutional capabilities traditionally associated with effective collective defense and collective security respond only to the most extreme consequences without necessarily assisting in the prevention of those consequences or the resolution of their causes. If NATO and the United Nations remain respectively committed to traditional approaches to collective defense and security, rejecting adaptation to new problems, their prospects are questionable. One commentator has contended that any system of collective security demands highly unique prerequisite conditions that are unlikely to occur under any circumstances; they will necessarily become even less likely to succeed in the face of the current changes in the global system.[54] Another argues that collective security institutions may not only fail to make constructive contributions, they may also aggravate the risks posed in already serious circumstances.[55] At the very least, these observations suggest the need for reconsideration of both the institutions and their conceptual foundations.

Conceptual Alternatives

Several recent authors have begun the task of reconsidering the institutional foundations upon which multilateral responses to issues of international security have been based. Their comments and criticisms offer differing prognoses for collective security and collective defense institutions. They may also offer insight into new sets of norms that may arise.

Joseph Nye

Joseph Nye has made some provocative observations that bear directly on the traditional assumptions and the new context.[56] According to Nye, both realists and liberals have tried to fit new situations into old paradigms. Realists continue to tout military power as the primary element of international power; they cite the Gulf War as their best evidence. Liberals, on the other hand, see Wilsonian elements emphasizing peoples and international institutions, relying on broad values and international law.[57]

Nye suggests an image of multilevel interdependence as his alternative.[58] He contends that the linkages between international actors vary depending on the level of analysis.

> No single hierarchy describes adequately a world politics with multiple structures. The distribution of power in world politics has become like a layer cake. The top military layer is largely unipolar, for there is no other military power comparable to the United States. The economic middle layer is tripolar and has been for two decades. The bottom layer of transnational interdependence shows a diffusion of power.[59]

At the unipolar military level, states are the principal actors, and the military power of the United States makes it dominant. At the economic top level, international institutions and groupings of state actors exercise predominant power. At the bottom, transnational interdependence blurs distinctions between domestic and foreign policies, making political parties and other national forces important arbiters of international policy.[60] Nye has described the interactions between participants on these different levels as reminiscent of "a three-dimensional chess game."[61]

Nye notes that some international institutions have begun to adjust to the range of values and actors implied by a system of multilevel interdependence. In particular, the United Nations has reacted to immediate problems with mechanisms that may prove well-adapted to a different and evolving global system.[62] These situational responses, forced by the necessity of responding to immediate crises in spite of anachronistic concepts and capabilities, may have nurtured a style of institutional learning that has some promise for the future.

Samuel Huntington

Another vision is offered by Samuel P. Huntington in a provocative recent. article.[63] He also argues that the state will lose pride of place as the determinative actor in global relations; however, he sees much larger groupings as playing a more important role. Huntington argues that *cultural identity* will provide the decisive criteria around which masses of human populations will organize themselves. As a result, civilizations become critical since "a civilization is . . . the highest cultural grouping of people and the broadest level of cultural identity people have short of that which distinguishes humans from other species."[64]

According to Huntington, the importance of civilizations grows from several factors.[65] First, they reflect basic real differences between the cultures of peoples. Second, increased interactions between people of differing civilizations have increased personal awareness of their differences. Third, social changes have unmoored people from local geographic identities. Fourth, the dominance of the West has forced non-Western civilizations to see a return to their roots as a means of preserving cultural identity. Fifth, compromise proves less viable when conflicts concern cultural characteristics rather than political differences. Finally, although economic regionalism is growing as a response to global competition, culturally-based economic entities may provide relatively greater opportunities for economic integration.

The most important implications of Huntington's analysis arise from his contention that "[t]he fault lines between civilizations are replacing the political and ideological boundaries of the Cold War as the flash points for crisis and bloodshed."[66] He asserts that "civilization commonality . . . is replacing political ideology and traditional balance of power considerations as the principal basis for cooperations and coalitions."[67] In the face of these trends, the actions of those Western states, cloaked in claims based upon supposedly "universal" values, become problematic. Huntington contends that "[t]he very phrase 'the world community' has become the euphemistic collective noun (replacing 'the Free World') to give global legitimacy to actions reflecting the interests of the United States and other Western powers."

Huntington briefly sets forth potential short and long term implications for the West and possible strategies for response, but he does not claim to be exhaustive.[68] He does indicate that states sharing the values and interests of Western civilization should recognize that states arising from other different civilizations need not and will not share the same perceptions. At the same time, Western states must recognize that groupings of states representing non-Western cultures will increase in power and relevance in all international contexts. Critical to this discussion, Huntington emphasizes that it is important for the West "to prevent escalation of local intercivilizational conflicts into major intercivilizational wars" and "to strengthen international institutions that reflect and legitimate Western interests and values and to promote the involvement of non-Western states in those institutions."

While these arguments differ dramatically, they all suggest reasons for the insufficiency of the traditional state-centric model.[69] They also suggest that many traditional norms incorporating liberal value assumptions may fail to address the cultural and ethnic identities that drive many contemporary conflicts. Nye suggests that as the varied entities of the system of multilevel interdependence evolve, so will the norms applicable to interactions between them. In that process, relationships between entities operating in different parts of the three-dimensional chess game will generate new and different principles. In contrast, Huntington implies that deeply rooted cultural difference may limit the degree to which those new and different general principles may be generated; he might conclude that pragmatic *ad hoc* responses may be the only practicable course. Part of that response capability involves reliance on international organizations.

Each of these discussions provides reasons for demanding flexibility and adaptability in any international organization that hopes to respond successfully to international crises. Whether or not the existing collective security and collective defense organizations offer that flexibility and adaptability remains to be seen. The next two sections will examine the United Nations and the NATO alliance with respect to their problems in responding to some of the problems that have arisen after the Cold War. To the extent that an institution can effectively identify, adopt and manage techniques and approaches beyond the traditional tools of diplomacy and military coercion, that institution may provide some useful contribution to future problems of international peace and security. Ultimately, cooperation between institutions may be the key to successful adaptation to the crises of the new world disorder.

UN Pressures

Although it may have reached new levels of respect among some of the states and peoples of the world, the U.N. now confronts entirely unanticipated stresses and pressures. The United Nations faces severe strains in responding to these new threats. The U.N. may have passed through a troubled adolescence to enter a period of maturity that could overwhelm it. Some of its prospective difficulties grow from the political compromises at the U.N.'s founding.

Limited Collective Security

Although it is common to characterize Chapter VII of the Charter as establishing a collective security process, those who negotiated the Charter had a more limited and pragmatic notion in mind.[70] They sought to insure that the enforcement process preserved freedom of action for the victors in the post-war world. In prospective crises where those victors had decided that they shared common interests, the collective enforcement procedures of Chapter VII would facilitate a unified response. On the other hand, whenever the interests of the principal powers differed, each retained a procedural device to prevent any collective action inconsistent with its interests. That weapon, the veto, permitted each power sufficient confidence that it could control the actions of the organization.

As Inis Claude noted, the United Nations collective enforcement system differed from traditional "balance of power" arrangements.[71] Balance of power described a system in which any disruptive action by any power would generate a hostile coalition among the other powers to maintain the status quo. The U.N. system enabled each of the victorious powers to prevent coalitions against its interests; collective enforcement could only occur when the five permanent members agreed that another actor had created a "threat to international peace and security." As between the major powers, balance of power politics remained intact. Through the United Nations, the victors created a system of limited collective security adapted to respond to threats of aggression while preserving the traditional coercive interplay when permanent members were involved.[72]

As a result, the United Nations collective security system allowed two classes of responses. If a minor power committed "aggression" within the unanimous consensus understanding, collective response will follow. However, if either a permanent member or its client-state exercised coercive power, the veto structure prevented the organization from attempting a necessarily futile intervention against a permanent member.

The Limits of Limited Collective Security

With continued problems in Iraq and new conflicts elsewhere, the optimism about the function of the United Nations that grew following the Gulf War has waned. Some of the Security Council's willingness to initiate new approaches has met with grudging support from nonwestern states. When the Security Council identified Kurdish repressions as subject to Security Council action, the resolution was adopted by only a slim margin.[73] There was an equally narrow margin of support for sanctions against Libya.[74] In addition, some states initially displayed either willingness to violate the sanctions[75] or opposition to their expansion.[76] Much of this dissatisfaction grows from doubts about the combination of military predominance and practical procedural control of the Security Council in the hands of the United States. With its new status as the sole superpower, the U.S. may be even more suspect in nonwestern eyes.

U.S. power and U.N. consensus have highlighted new questions about the Security Council process.[77] Consensus among the permanent five raises greater difficulties with the apparent expansion of the Security Council's mandate by redefining threats to international peace and security. Continued resort by the Council to these nontraditional initiatives may lead other U.N. member states to express serious reservations about the Security Council's actions.[78]

The Problems of New Operations

Renewed discussion of the United Nations and the daunting tasks that it has undertaken have begun to outline the scope of the necessary tasks. The Security Council Summit and the *Agenda for Peace* report attempted to address the issues raised by the new range of responsibilities on the organization's agenda.[79] Although many concerned with the United Nations both inside and outside of the organization are addressing these questions, the issues remain in doubt.

In spite of these doubts, the United Nations has undertaken an historic number of peacekeeping and humanitarian relief operations since the end of the Cold War.[80] Peacekeeping initially developed as an emergency mechanism to cope with international crises by facilitating the termination of hostilities. Because of the unwillingness of the superpowers to allow the development of the operational capability contemplated during Charter drafting, *ad hoc* designation of small operational monitoring and buffer forces became the only possible option for crisis response. During practical evolution, those responsible for peacekeeping have elaborated a specific set of prerequisites for initiation of operations. These have included "consent of the parties; continuing strong support of the Security Council; a clear and practicable mandate; non-use of force except in the last resort and in self-defense; willingness of troop contributors to furnish military forces; and willingness of member states to make available requisite financing."[81]

Within the past two years, controversial operations have occurred in Bosnia and Somalia. In both cases, substantial numbers of troops have been deployed in situations that involve either active participation in ground combat or exposure to risks from the ongoing actions of hostile combatants. In both cases, the conflict involved combatants who were within the traditional boundaries of states. These operations have strayed from some of the prerequisites rules of peacekeeping. In Bosnia, even though the national government gave consent, those parties made up of local rebel military forces have opposed U.N. peacekeeping operations, firing on them on occasion. In Somalia, no state existed to extend consent, and although negotiations with local warlords allowed initial agreement, open combat has ensued between U.N. contingents and the forces of a local warlord. These events have raised a number of questions about peacekeeping and U.N. operations. Although the *Agenda for Peace* report anticipated a number of the potential problems, the United Nations may have ingrained institutional problems that limit its operational effectiveness when operations move outside the narrow scope of peacekeeping.

Because of limitations inherent in the peacekeeping paradigm, the United Nations may face serious difficulties in responding to the sorts of internal and ethnic conflicts that have broken out with the collapse of the superpower blocs.[82] When peacekeeping operations serve a role that is primarily political, allowing parties that have committed themselves to negotiated solutions to finalize detailed agreements, the absence of detailed command and control procedures has limited importance.[83] However, operations that require that U.N. forces stand ready to employ military force in the enforcement of the edicts of the security Council cannot allow such lax operational control.[84] The essential criteria for effective multilateral application of military force include: resolute political leadership; sophisticated and flexible command structures responsive to the particular political limitations suffered by some partners; and operational planning capabilities organs able to coordinate forces having varied capabilities and skills.[85] Few of the essential skills for the conduct of such operations currently exist in the United Nations.[86] Until those skills are developed, the organization runs significant risks in initiating new operations that move beyond the narrow parameters of traditional peacekeeping.[87]

Sources of Risks for the United Nations

The United Nations stands at a crossroads. A number of obstacles stand in the way of creative initiatives to new classes of problems. Critics have consistently noted the inefficiency and inertia that characterize much of the United Nations system. The enormous numbers of actors who participate in its processes may provide both the greatest hope and the most prodigious burden confronting the United Nations. Increasing membership on the Security Council may further frustrate the speed of crisis responses. Financing the activities of the United Nations may prove to involve enormous free-rider problems.

These problems may inhibit the United Nations from adapting to the changing international system.

Institutional inertia within both the United Nations and national governments can frustrate the initiative of those facing real problems on the ground. Both existing governments and groups seeking self-determination hold commitments to the political dimensions of the concept of sovereignty. Those commitments will limit their willingness to accept new United Nations initiatives. Recent discussion of "micronationalism" indicates some of the dimensions of this problem.[88]

The United Nations has indicated concern for addressing these issues, but many questions remain unanswered. The *Agenda for Peace* report by Secretary-General Boutros-Ghali addresses several strategies that are both old and new. Peacekeeping, a traditional activity for the U.N., receives theoretical reinforcement from enhanced proposals for peacemaking and preventive diplomacy.[89] Even with these approaches, however, the report adopts much of the state-centric image that accompanied the formation of the United Nations.[90] By failing to recognize that states are not the sole participants in the international system of peace and war, the report misses the opportunity to address new options.[91] In addition, it fails to develop the concept of "preventive diplomacy" in ways that offer adequate promise for serving the critical early warning functions necessary for United Nations effectiveness.[92] The *Agenda for Peace* report has sparked significant debate on important and relevant issues. Unless member states of the United Nations come to understand the changes in the nature of the international system and of the types of participants active in that system, they will continue to respond with time-honored and irrelevant remedies to increasingly serious international ailments.

Beyond the serious questions that have been raised about the ability of the United Nations to exercise effective command and control of operations that move beyond peacekeeping, the United Nations confronts enormous challenges in adjusting to newly perceived relations of power and influence. First, although some may doubt it, the U.N. may be responding as effectively as possible to current conflicts and humanitarian crises. A more important question involves whether those meaningful responses will constitute effective resolutions of the underlying causes of conflict. The prospects for those resolutions will turn on whether the member states of the United Nations can address the question of the contemporary purposes of an institution established in a different geopolitical era. So far, the member states have not confronted these issues forthrightly.

Second, some reforms of institutional structure are necessary to preserve the legitimacy of the organizations. Just as the credibility of the organization at its founding turned on its consistency with the contemporary distribution of political power and importance, reforms are necessary to adapt the organization to the contemporary order of political power and importance. However, any reforms will fail unless they address purposes and objectives which (1) recognize the changing nature of the international system and its types of participants, and also (2) gain serious commitments by member states. Many initiatives might be suggested relating to the structure of the Security Council or the relationship of the Council to the General Assembly. The particular approach is less important than the necessary result of providing all member states with a stake in the conflict resolution efforts of the organization.

Finally, the question of U.N. financing will be critical. As the *Agenda for Peace* report notes, some of the greatest obstacles faced by the organization involve the financing of new undertakings.[93] A comparison of recent United Nations efforts in Angola and Namibia shows that thoughtful and original planning combined with a commitment of adequate resources can make the critical difference.[94] Whether or not the United Nations faces institutional overload is partly a question of financing; it is also a question of institutional organization and capabilities. However, unless there is adequate financing, the need to generate *ad hoc* responses to immediate crisis situations will prevent any of the systematic institutional reforms and the development of operational capabilities that could enhance the organization's long-term effectiveness. Without resolving the financial question, the United Nations does face the serious risk that it will fail to live up to the hopes that blossomed at the beginning of the post-Cold War era.

Without doubt, the United Nations faces a range of very difficult problems. However, the United Nations is not alone in facing serious jeopardy from the vast changes on the international scene. The North Atlantic Treaty Organization faces many similar difficulties, some of them growing from the adherence to similar foundational conceptions of security. Unfortunately, NATO may also lack the capability to adapt to new understandings of the world.

Problems for NATO[95]

The end of the Cold War has been credibly touted as the best evidence of the success of the NATO idea. However, the narrowness of NATO's purposes and institutional structures has caused serious difficulties with attempts to adjust to newly-perceived international arrangements. Perhaps for that reason, the new international order may provide NATO with obstacles to which it cannot adjust. After maturing in the face of a stable bipolar order and adapting specifically to the demands of that arrangement, NATO may find it difficult to adjust to a radically different world. NATO's success may have marked the beginning of its demise by destroying its purpose. In NATO's case, the aftermath of success has shown the limits of the single-minded institutional purposes and structures established to implement collective defense.

Historically, reaching a political consensus on responses to a perceived Soviet conventional or nuclear threat proved to be relatively simple. While debate abounded about Soviet intentions, the existence of a substantial Soviet military capability could be easily observed. Military analysts could reach agreement on basic strategies for responding to that perceived capability. The military establishments of NATO member states could respond by providing forces that fit within that basic strategic plan. The purpose of the alliance combined with perceived strategic necessity to provide for the development of a dedicated collective defense structure. With the disappearance of the Soviet Union, those unifying verities evaporated. Without the threat scenario provided by a Soviet monolith, new challenges to European peace and security became apparent. Ethnic and nationalist conflict between and within former East-bloc states has caused significant concerns. Unfortunately, recognition of these conflicts has not led NATO officials to propose any common response. In fact, until the NATO summit in June 1992, most European officials expressed the belief that the North Atlantic Treaty prohibited deployment of NATO-controlled forces outside their defensive theater.

This new strategic uncertainty in NATO has important practical consequences. Alliance military planners have developed their estimates of minimum force structures based on contingency plans that identify the capabilities necessary to respond to the most probable threats. Rapid changes in the current international scene makes the development of any contingency plans for deployment of NATO forces a practical impossibility. NATO planners encounter additional frustrating limitations since they must avoid politically unacceptable threat scenarios that might appear to involve the special interests of a NATO member state. The resulting plans have little utility for either analysts identifying necessary military capabilities or officers preparing for possible operational deployments.

As NATO members confront question about their collective ability to respond to new security threats, eastern European states have few doubts. NATO's former eastern European enemies are seeking to join the collective security regime. In response, NATO has developed an ambitious liaison program with the defense ministries of most of the former Warsaw Pact member states and quite a few of the republics of the former Soviet Union. Eastern European civilian and military visitors have expressed the desire to become associated with the western alliance. NATO officials cannot reasonably believe that these former Warsaw Pact members see NATO as a threat; in fact, many former Pact members see NATO as their salvation, as the instrument that allowed their political liberation.

In contrast, many traditional supporters now wonder whether the collective defense alliance still has utility. Changes on the European scene have led to some dissatisfaction with NATO. Voters in member countries who witnessed the collapse of the eastern bloc as they experienced economic recessions have begun to ask whether the military infrastructure of NATO provides services worth the enormous costs. Opposition politicians pose questions challenging leaders who continue to support NATO. Academic specialists in international security matters publish articles questioning the continued viability of the Atlantic alliance as an institution. Some suggest the elimination of NATO in favor of other alternative security arrangements such as the Western European Union or the Conference on Security and Cooperation in Europe (CSCE). To maintain their relevance, alliance leaders have recently concluded that NATO may now undertake peacekeeping missions under the auspices of CSCE and the United Nations, endeavors which would involve unspecified initiatives in unpredictable situations. This function could not stand in greater contrast with the single-minded task that confronted NATO for more than forty years.

NATO and Yugoslavia

The situation in Yugoslavia has shaken the confidence of a range of European institutions. Because of changes in the east, the practical borders of Europe have expanded to include culturally different, economically depressed, and ethnically divided states. The Yugoslav conflict has provided chilling evidence of the difficulties that confront the new Europe. Differences in national policies have severely inhibited the European reaction to fighting between the former Yugoslav republics. At the first assertions of independent status by Slovenia and Croatia, some European powers supported full sovereignty for the breakaway republics while others warned of possible dire consequences of efforts to form separate sovereign states.

None of the past institutional experiences of NATO prepared it for the actual and potential carnage. The resulting fighting in Croatia and Bosnia-Hercegovina led to some officials to express collective self-doubt about the readiness of NATO to play a responsible foreign policy role in a more general arena.[96] In fact, some NATO officials have questioned whether, absent U.S. leadership, the European democracies can exercise the collective political will to undertake risky actions in response to collective security threats.

Although NATO has recently offered assistance to other organizations pursuing remedies in Yugoslavia, NATO found it very difficult to decide independently upon appropriate responses. One principal reason for reluctance grows from the "out-of-area" constraint that has limited NATO's response to events outside of Western Europe.[97] NATO's original mandate limited its activities to threats to the territorial security of the parties in Europe.[98] The territorial limitation of the NATO commitment resulted from American fear potential involvement in colonial wars. This provision has led to a tradition of rejection of any NATO commitment to engagements outside of the NATO area.[99]   That rejection led to controversy during the Gulf conflict, when most member countries made some contribution to the coalition even though NATO could not formally participate in Desert Storm.[100]

NATO has begun to recognize that "[t]he challenges we will face in this new Europe cannot be comprehensively addressed by one institution alone, but only in a framework of interlocking institutions."[101]   The constraint imposed by NATO's territorial limitation has been weakened.[102] However, political realities have limited the prospects for NATO to undertake independent peacekeeping operations.[103]   Beyond these difficulties, consensus action has been inhibited by the complications involved in effectively addressing long term perspectives on the future of Yugoslavia.   NATO has not developed independent policy on this or any other ethnic/nationalist conflict.[104]

NATO has undertaken a surprising range of peacekeeping and other operations in the context of the Yugoslav conflict.[105] In fact, the siege of Sarajevo has been ameliorated as a result of NATO's preparations to enforce United Nations Security Council Resolution 836 calling for protection of United Nations forces in Bosnia.[106]   These latest involvements may offer the route by which the capabilities of NATO are brought to bear on contemporary international problems.[107]   While the top diplomatic levels of NATO may suffer from redundancy, the military staff and operational capabilities may find usefulness through other organizations.   In any event, the norms and values that drove NATO during the Cold War offer much less help in the current period.   NATO in its traditional form, reflecting single minded attention to a massive aggressive threat, may be doomed to irrelevance.   However, NATO may continue to play an important role in conjunction with other international organizations in arrangements where each offers to play a role suitable to that organizations structures, norms and capabilities.

Conclusion: The Challenge of New World Disorder

Continuing turbulence in the international scene should prevent any reasonable spectator from prognosticating with confidence.   However, a few observations might be forgiven.

Comparing NATO and the United Nations, I would suggest a few hypotheses.

The initial concept of limited collective security fell upon the obstacle of superpower competition, frustrating all involved with the United Nations for the first four decades of its existence. During that time, creative initiatives were required to accomplish any progress at all. For example, the peacekeeping practice of the United Nations evolved without specific authority under the Charter.[108] In addition, the United Nations has largely accomplished the decolonization tasks through norms and procedures not contemplated at the formation of the Trusteeship Council.[109]

This institutional flexibility and originality may provide a foundation for future responses to a world characterized by multilevel interdependence. Through a large network of institutions which involve states, international organizations, national and ethnic groupings, nongovernmental organizations, and a range of other participants, the United Nations system may be comparatively well positioned to adapt to the demands of an evolving international system. Unfortunately, anecdotal instances of resourceful crisis responses offer very thin grounds for optimism. Anyone expressing optimism about the United Nations system should be subject to serious challenge.

Despite these risks, I suggest that the United Nations holds some promise for adapting to new situations. The characteristics developed for responding to early and continuing challenges to the fundamental structures and purposes of the organization may offer some flexibility. However, that promise obviously has limitations. Unfortunately, given its mandate, the United Nations has no option but to deal with these new situations; limitations in bureaucratic effectiveness, representative legitimacy, financing, and command and control may limit its efforts. Under these circumstances, the United Nations any need to rely on institutional partners to remedy its weaknesses. NATO may prove to be a valuable partner in certain circumstances.

NATO also faces difficulties coping with the range of global changes that have occurred. While NATO's defensive alliance may have been successful, that success resulted at least partially from the single-minded commitment of its members to a specific and identifiable goal. That goal virtually dictated a strategy for its accomplishment, and that strategy allowed the evolution of a powerful institution specifically adapted for accomplishing tasks identified by the strategy. The collective defense alliance adapted so precisely to its task that it became overly specialized. The specific capabilities of military operational and staff units attached to NATO may have utility in other situations, and the capabilities developed within NATO for multinational operation may have other applications. However, the central institutional image of the world has disappeared, and the organization faces a continuing struggle to preserve its usefulness.[110]

The Bosnian conflict demonstrates some of NATO's limitations as well as its possibilities. NATO has not been forced by its mandate to become involved in situations like Yugoslavia. Until recently, it has fulfilled its mandate of providing collective defense for the western democracies without engaging in any activities outside of immediate areas essential to the territorial defense of alliance members. That limitation has prevented NATO from playing any formal role in important international conflicts.[111]

However, recent initiatives demonstrate that NATO is attempting to develop a constructive role for itself as part of an interlocking network of institutions capable of responding to new threats to international security. While the structures and processes developed by NATO in accomplishing its central purpose may have left it unable to respond immediately and independently to some new international threats, the organization has undertaken self-critical efforts to broaden its shared understanding of the nature of relevant international threats. Beyond this, cooperation with other multilateral organizations may allow collective institutional adaptation to the new world disorder. Although the traditional norms and principles of NATO may recede in importance, NATO's military forces and logistical, intelligence and planning capabilities may serve important purposes. In particular, these changes may allow NATO and the United Nations to work together toward common solutions to shared threats, relying on complementary capabilities where necessary. These institutions must develop the ability to function jointly; the range of problems to be faced calls for new and original approaches.

Cooperation between NATO and the United Nations may offer only limited potential. NATO is a European organization. Several of its members are former colonial powers whose role in conflicts outside of Europe may raise questions of legitimacy similar to those now faced by the Untied Nations Security Council. These questions of legitimacy may prevent NATO from providing peacekeeping or any other capabilities in conflicts involving less developed countries. However, the planning, logistics, and intelligence procedures of NATO could provide models for United Nations operations; even if units from NATO countries may be suspect, NATO-based individuals offering specific expertise may still play a useful role.

Ultimately, cooperation between NATO and the United Nations may offer the best potential for both organizations. The U.N., as a universal organization concerned with a broad range of global questions and problems, may make useful contributions to the new types of problems leading to post-Cold War conflicts. NATO, on the other hand, may offer many of the specific operational capabilities that the U.N. is lacking in its efforts to undertake complex peacekeeping and peace enforcement operations. Neither of these institutions can afford to venture into the new world disorder with initiatives based on obsolete images of the international system; without serious adaptation, failure looms unavoidably. In contrast, shared efforts to adapt to the changing system, relying on the relevant capacities and understandings of each organization, may offer some hope for constructive joint contributions to the enhancement of international peace and security.

During the 1960s, many young people read a book by Alan Watts called *The Wisdom of Insecurity*.[112] The thesis of the work was that uncertainty forces creative responses and growth. Conversely, life without insecurity inhibits opportunities for development. Beyond this, efforts to guarantee security will fail; since change is inescapable, insecurity is inevitable. Consequently, acceptance of insecurity is wisdom.

Comparison of the United Nations and NATO could lead to similar conclusions. NATO maintained the *status quo* in Europe through the creation of an effective and elaborate military and diplomatic institution. That alliance preserved a high level of security in Europe, allowing rich and expanding economies which provided a telling contrast with eastern neighbors. Ultimately, with the collapse of the Soviet bloc, NATO witnessed the withering of the threat that provided its foundational principle. While its capabilities may be called upon in crisis situations, NATO's fundamental success may have doomed its traditional incarnation.

The United Nations has struggled since its foundation against challenges to its fundamental norms and principles. Some of the formal members of the great power club of 1945 have suffered diminution in their power, while nonmembers have gained vast importance. Superpower competition, after frustrating the organization for more than forty years, has disappeared because only one of them remains. Even the definition of international power has shifted toward multilevel interdependence in ways not contemplated in 1945. The United Nations, after enduring these changes, has entered a new era of initiative and activity. However, much of those activities may face critical difficulties, raising questions in critical situations about the norms and the institutional capabilities of the United Nations.

While there can be no confidence in ultimate success, the U.N. could begin to accomplish many of its objectives. The prospects of success would be greatly enhanced if the U.N. could take advantage of the sorts of operational capabilities that NATO has already developed. By the same token, NATO could remain relevant to questions of global security by institutionalizing its nascent understandings of the changed international security agenda. Radical change in the global system will force both institutions to examine the fundamental assumptions upon which they have based themselves. If significant success takes place for these organizations, both NATO and the U.N. may have learned wisdom through insecurity.

Notes to Collective Security and Collective Defense

1. See Joseph S. Nye, Jr., "What New World Order?" *Foreign Affairs* (Spring 1992), 83-96.

2. We may be learning the lessons of postmodernism:

> The postmodern school of thought conceives of knowledge as always mediated by our social, cultural, linguistic and historical circumstances, and it will thus vary as those circumstances change. The truth, consequently, can never be transparent to us; it is and must always be a social construction, one made even more opaque by the mediation of language, a system of communication inherently incapable of capturing reality.

Peter C. Schank, "Understanding Postmodern Thought and its Implications for Statutory Interpretation," 65 *Southern California Law Review* (1992), 2507.

3. See Hayward R. Alker, Jr., Thomas J. Bierstecker, and Takashi Inoguchi, "From Imperial Power Balancing to People's Wars: Searching for Order in the Twentieth Century," in James Der Derian and Michael J. Shapiro, eds., *International/Intertextual Relations: Postmodern Readings of World Politics* (1989), 135-162.

4. Many commentators have struggled to define "international security" issues. Since I do not intend to engage in that extensive debate, I use the terms global security and international security interchangeably. For purposes of this discussion, I prefer to focus on situations that risk generating large-scale violence which has some implications for actors outside the traditional boundaries of the state within which that violence is most likely. These cases need not be limited to situations involving interstate violence; similarly, the relevant actors should not be limited to states alone. Obviously, a number of international dangers are omitted by this characterization. Environmental threats come to mind immediately. However, comparisons of NATO and the United Nations would become unmanageable unless areas of common concern provide an organizing dimension.

5. Sheik Ali defines collective security as "[a] means of restraining aggression and ending breaches of peace by agreement of a body of nations to take common action." Sheik Ali, *The International Organizations and*

World Order Dictionary (1992), 35-36. Formalized ideas of collective security began with the Treaty of Versailles. Edmund Osmanczyk, *Encyclopedia of the United Nations and International Agreements* (2nd. ed. 1990), 175-176. Larry and Marina Finkelstein note similar ideas offered by political philosophers centuries earlier. Marina Finkelstein and Larry Finkelstein, "The Future and Collective Security: An Essay," in Marina Finkelstein and Larry Finkelstein, eds., *Collective Security* (1966), 255-273.

6. Charter of the United Nations. Done at San Francisco, June 26, 1945. Entered into force, Oct. 24, 1945; for the United States, Oct. 24, 1945. 59 Stat. 1031, T.S. No. 993, 3 Bevans 1153, 1976 Y.B.U.N. 1043 (hereafter, "the United Nations Charter" or "the Charter").

7. Sheik Ali, 35.

8. Evan Luard, *A History of the United Nations: The Years of Western Domination, 1945-1955* (1982).

9. Mohammed Ayoob, "Squaring the Circle: Collective Security in the System of States," in Thomas G. Weiss, ed., *Collective Security in a Changing World* (Boulder: Lynne Reiner, 1993), 48.

10. Done at Washington, D.C., April 4, 1949. Entered into force, Aug. 24, 1949; for the United States, Aug. 24, 1949. 63 Stat 2241, T.I.A.S. No. 1964, 4 Bevans 828, U.N.T.S. 243 (hereafter, the "NATO Treaty").

11. The NATO Treaty does commit member states to refrain from the threat or use of force in their international relations and to settle any international disputes by peaceful means. NATO Treaty, Art. 1.

12. S.C. Res. 660 (1990), August 2, 1990.

13. Thomas Franck, *Nation Against Nation: What Happened to the U.N. Dream and What the U.S. Can Do About It* (New York: Oxford University Press, 1985), 6-24.

14. Ibid., 25-44.

15. Although post-Cold War optimism about the United Nations results largely from the ending of this sort of bilateral manipulation, the current controversy over the Palestinian exiles and Security Council Res. 799 shows that the bilateral manipulations have not completely disappeared. See Clyde

Haberman, "Israel's Highest Court Upholds The Deportation of Palestinians," *New York Times* (January 29, 1993).

16. Michael Howard, "The UN and International Security," in A. Roberts and B. Kingsbury, eds., *United Nations, Divided World: The UN's Participation in International Relations* (Clarendon: Oxford, 1989), 45.

17. Ibid.

18. Ibid., 35.

19. Roberts and Kingsbury, "Introduction: The UN's Role in a Divided World," in A. Roberts and B. Kingsbury, eds., 2.

20. Ibid.

21. Abraham Sofaer, "Terrorism and the Law," 64 *Foreign Affairs* (1986), 901, 906. Abraham Sofaer served as Legal Advisor to the Department of State during the Reagan and Bush Administrations.

22. Alan Keyes, "Fixing the U.N.," *National Interest* (Summer 1986), 12, 16-18. Alan Keyes served as Assistant Secretary of State for International Organizations. His responsibilities included United Nations affairs.

23. Daniel Patrick Moynihan, *Loyalties* (1984), 42.

24. See Thomas G. Weiss and Meryl A. Kessler, "Moscow's U.N. Policy," *Foreign Affairs* (Summer 1990), 94; Text of Gorbachev's to the 43rd Session of the United Nations General Assembly, TASS, December 7, 1988.

25. Text of President Bush's Address to Joint Session of Congress, *New York Times* (September 12, 1990).

26. Excerpts From Baker Testimony on U.S. and Gulf, *New York Times* (September 9, 1990).

27. Ibid.

28. Ibid.

29. See the text of Joint Statement, *New York Times* (September 10, 1990).

30. Address of Soviet Foreign Minister Eduard Shevardnadze to the United Nations General Assembly, NEXIS, *Federal News Service* (September 25, 1990).

31. Security Council Summit Statement, U.N. Document S/23500, January 31, 1992 .

32. These arguments were usually based on Article 2(7).

33. Security Council Resolution 688, SC Res. 688, April 5, 1991.

34. *Report of the Secretary-General on an Agenda for Peace: Preventive Diplomacy, Peacemaking and Peace-Keeping*, U.N. Doc. S/24111, June 17, 1992. See Boutros Boutros-Ghali, "Empowering the United Nations," *Foreign Affairs* (Winter 1992/1993), 88-102.

35. The American opposition to the French and British assault on the Suez Canal in 1956 provided one of these crises. Another occurred with the French withdrawal from the NATO military command structure in 1966. John Newhouse, *War and Peace in the Nuclear Age* (1988), 200.

36. For a discussion of regime theory, see Edwin M. Smith, "Understanding Dynamic Obligations: Arms Control Agreements," 64 *Southern California Law Review*, 1549, 1591-1593.

Regime principles constitute a consistent set of theoretical axioms and ethical beliefs about the manner in which the world functions. Regime norms specify general standards of behavior for actors. Regime rules refer to specific prescriptions for behavior, while regime decision-making procedures consist of mechanisms for evaluating whether action within a specific context complies with the relevant rules. Stephen Krasner, "Structural Causes and Regime Consequences: Regimes as Intervening Variables," in Stephen Krasner, ed., *International Regimes* (1983), 2. See also Stephen Krasner, *Structural Conflict: The Third World Against Global Liberalism* (1985), 4.

The basic character and goal structure of a regime are defined by its principles and norms. The formal legal structure of the regime may partially reflect its norms, rules or decision procedures. Variations in rules and decision-making procedures indicate changes within the continuing regime.

However, substantial modification of the principles and norms of a regime reveal fundamental variations of the regime itself.

37. See Schultz, "Shaping American Foreign Policy: New Realities and New Ways of Thinking," 63 *Foreign Affairs* (1985), 705, 706, 709-710.

38. See Alan K. Henrikson, "The Creation of the North Atlantic Alliance," in John Reichert and Steven Strum, *American Defense Policy* (1982 ed.), 296, 298. In fact, the attempt to form a collective balance of power may be a general characteristic of alliances. Stephen Walt, *The Origins of Alliances* (1987), 263.

39. Alan K. Henrikson, 310.

40. North Atlantic Treaty, Art. 5, 63 Stat. 2241, T.I.A.S. No. 1964.

41. North Atlantic Treaty, Art. 11.

42. North Atlantic Treaty, Art. 9; Alan K. Henrikson, *supra* note at 311-312; Donald R. Cotter, "Peacetime Operations: Safety and Security," in Ashton B. Carter, John D. Steinbruner, and Charles A. Zraket, eds., *Managing Nuclear Operations* (1987), 17, 39-40.

43. Discussions of "failed states" and "trusteeships" cannot help but heighten these fears. See Gerald Helman and Stephen Ratner, "Saving Failed States," *Foreign Policy* (Winter 1992-1993), 3-20.

44. Avner Cohen and Marvin Miller, "How to Think About—and Implement—Nuclear Arms Control in the Middle East," *Washington Quarterly* (Spring 1993), 98.

45. Ibid.

46. Ibid.

47. Ibid.

48. See Daniel Patrick Moynihan, *Pandaemonium: Ethnicity in International Politics* (Oxford: Oxford University Press, 1993). Francis Fukuyama predicts that "the future promises many new instances of painful ethnic conflicts" which will require new approaches to foreign policy.

Francis Fukuyama, "The Beginning of Foreign Policy: America Confronts the Post-Cold War World," *The New Republic* (August 17, 1992), 8-9.

49. Robin Wright, "Ethnic Strife Owes More to Present Than to History," *Los Angeles Times* (June 8, 1993).

50. *Los Angeles Times*, June 8, 1993.

51. John H. Jackson, *Restructuring the GATT System* (New York: Council on Foreign Relations, 1990); Stephen C. Neff, *Friends But Not Allies: Economic Nationalism and the Law of Nations* (New York: Columbia University Press, 1990).

52. See Jagdish Bhagwati, "The Diminished Giant Syndrome; How Declinism Drives Trade Policy," *Foreign Affairs* (Spring 1993), 23.

53. See Robert Rothstein, "Democracy, Conflict, and Development in the Third World," *Washington Quarterly* (Spring 1991), 43.

54. Henry Kissinger has written:

> the doctrine of collective security is irrelevant to all but the most overpowering challenges to international order. The twin assumptions of collective security—that nations perceive each threat in the same way and are prepared to run identical risks—simply do not apply in most foreseeable situations.

Henry Kissinger, "What Kind of New World Order?" *Washington Post* (December 3, 1991).

55. See Richard K. Betts, "Systems of Peace or Causes of War? Collective Security, Arms Control and the New Europe," *International Security* (Summer 1992), 5-43.

56. Joseph R. Nye, Jr.

57. Ibid.

58. Ibid.

59. Ibid.

60. Nye described the operation of transnational interdependence:

> To cite a few examples: private actors in global capital markets constrain the way interest rates can be used to manage the American economy; the transnational spread of technology increases the destructive capacities of otherwise poor and weak states; and a number of issues on the international agenda—drug trade, AIDS, migration, global warming—have deep societal roots in more than one country and flow across borders largely outside of governmental control. Since military means are not very effective in coping with such problems, no great power, the United States included, will be able to solve them alone.

According to Nye, the diffusion of international power is a central characteristic of the current order. See Joseph S. Nye, Jr., *Bound to Lead: The Changing Nature of American Power* (1990), 173-201.

61. Speech delivered to the American Society of International Law, March 31, 1993, Washington D.C. (forthcoming in the Proceedings of the 87th Annual Meeting of the American Society of International Law).

62. Ibid. He notes collective responses in the area of human rights that have gone beyond traditional Westphalian norms of sovereignty, particularly when threats to international order are implicated. He also notes actions by regional organizations. He specifically suggests enhancing U.N. capabilities for independent response, including the formation of a rapid deployment force.

63. Samuel P. Huntington, "The Clash of Civilizations," *Foreign Affairs* (Summer 1993), 22-49.

64. Ibid., 24.

65. Ibid., 25-29.

66. Ibid., 29.

67. Ibid., 35.

68. Ibid., 48-49.

69. While Nye and Huntington offer two important views on the changing international order and is implications for states. However, others have been omitted because of considerations of space. Important and illuminating arguments have been offered by James N. Rosenau and John Ruggie. James N. Rosenau, *Turbulence in World Politics: A Theory of Change and Continuity* (Princeton: Princeton University Press 1990); John G. Ruggie, ed., *Multilateralism Matters: The Theory and Praxis of an Institutional Form* (New York: Columbia University Press 1993).

70. See R. Hilderbrand, *Dumbarton Oaks: The Origins of the United Nations and the Search for Postwar Security* (1990); Inis Claude, "The Management of Power in the Changing United Nations," reprinted in R. Falk, et al., *The United Nations and a Just World Order* (1991), 143-152; Marina Finkelstein and Larry Finkelstein.

71. See Inis Claude, 146-150. For a description of the post-Cold War context that proceeds from balance of power assumptions, see Henry Kissinger, 54.

72. Some of the problems involved in viewing Desert Storm as a pattern for future collective enforcement flow from the post-Cold War merger of those two classes of responses. The United States, the preeminent power, initiated coercive measures against Iraq which preserved vital American interests as they also responded to the multilateral consensus. Little remained of balance-of-power politics that could limit American action. Some claimed that the United States "hijacked" the Security Council. See Mouat, "Prestige High, UN Looks Stronger," *Christian Science Monitor* (March 11, 1991); Friedman, "UN United, Divided By U.S.' New Role," *Newsday* (July 29, 1991). Because the protection of the vital interests of the United States merged with collective international enforcement against Iraq, American claims to justification appeared tainted by self-interest, generating ambivalent responses.

73. While ten nations voted in favor of Resolution 688, Cuba, Yemen and Zimbabwe opposed the resolution, and China and India abstained.

74. The difficulty faced by the United States under the present circumstances is demonstrated by the controversy surrounding Security Council Resolution 748 imposing sanctions on Libya for failing to extradite individuals accused of terrorist bombings of aircraft. S.C.Res. 748 (1992). That resolution was adopted with a bare one vote margin with five members of the Security Council abstaining, including one permanent member. The frailty of the supporting consensus for that resolution shows that collective

security norms undergirding the Charter may be too brittle to permit broad expansion to cover new threats.

75. United Press International, "Sources Say Syria May Resume Flights to Libya," *NEXIS* (April 18, 1992), Current File.

76. Commentators expect a number of European states to indicate serious reservations about any broader sanctions involving Libyan oil exports. Associated Press, "Sanctions on Libya Begin: Jets Turned Back, Envoys Sent Home," *Chicago Tribune* (April 16, 1992).

77. Edward C. Luck and Tobi Trister Gati, "Whose Collective Security" *Washington Quarterly* (Spring 1992), 43. Unless the U.S. recognizes the difficulty of claiming its actions to be legitimate, it risks reactivating a pure balance of power system with itself as the power to be resisted by a broad coalition. Since military power faces ever declining utility in today's world, U.S. ability to accomplishing its goals by acting in isolation may be diminishing. Robert Tucker and David Hendrickson, *Imperial Temptations: The New World Order and America's Purpose* (1991), 14-17.

78. Most commentators indicate that the willingness of the membership of the United Nations to go along with the Somali relief operation grew because of the absence of a traditional government in Somalia. Some have drawn comparison to Sudan, a neighboring country where the traditional government is fighting a civil war with means that many consider genocidal. There appears to be no move afoot for military intervention to provide relief the civilians in southern Sudan.

79. See *Agenda for Peace*, *supra* note . For criticisms, see Thomas G. Weiss, "New Challenges for UN Military Operations: Implementing an Agenda for Peace," *Washington Quarterly* (Winter 1993).

80. For a useful survey of these activities, see Weiss, *supra*.

81. Ibid., (citing Sir Brian Urquhart).

82. John Mackinlay, "The Requirement for a Multinational Enforcement Capability," in Thomas G. Weiss, *supra* note, 139-151.

83. Ibid., 142.

84. The successful conduct of Operation Desert Storm may have ben possible only because the United Nations did not control the military decisionmaking process. See ibid., 144-145.

85. Ibid., 145.

86. Ibid., 146-147.

87. A number of authors have suggested courses that might be followed. See ibid., 149; Weiss, *supra* note 64-65; Jarat Chopra and John Mackinlay, "Future Multinational Military Operations," *Washington Quarterly* (Summer 1992), 124-155.

88. Secretary-General Boutros-Ghali has adopted the term: "The narrow nationalism that would oppose or disregard the norms of a stable international order and the micronationalism that resists healthy economic or political integration can destruct a peaceful global existence." Federal News Service, State Department Briefing, *United Nations Security Council Summit Opening Addresses*, Friday, January 31, 1992 (comments of Secretary-General Boutros-Ghali). See also Oscar Schachter, "Sovereignty and Threats to Peace," in Thomas G. Weiss, *supra* note, 37.

89. "Agenda for Peace," *supra* note .

90. The Secretary-General, while recognizing the limits of sovereignty, stated in the report that "[t]he foundation-stone of this work is and must remain the State. Respect for its fundamental sovereignty and integrity are crucial to any common international progress." Weiss offers an impressive number of forceful criticisms of the report. Thomas G. Weiss, *supra* note, 59-60.

91. Ibid.

92. See Michael G. Scheffer, "Preventive Diplomacy, Early Warning Systems, The Evolving Global System and United Nations Reform," in W. A. Andy Knight and Keith Drause, eds., *United Nations Reform for the Twenty-First Century* (forthcoming).

93. Boutros Boutros-Ghali, *supra* note 94-95. See Shijuro Ogata and Paul Volker, *Financing an Effective United Nations: A Report of the Independent Advisory Group on U.N. Financing* (The Ford Foundation, February 1993).

94. Ibid.

95. Many of the observations in this section result from discussions conducted at NATO in May, 1992. A description of that trip was published previously. See Edwin M. Smith, "NATO and the European Community: Troubled Transitions," *USC LAW* (Fall 1992), 2-11.

96. Craig Whitney, "NATO's Leadership Gap," *New York Times* (May 29, 1993).

97. David C. Morrison, "Beyond NATO," *National Journal* (February 23, 1991), 452.

98. See text following note 40. Article 4 of the NATO Treaty commits the parties to "consult together whenever, in the opinion of any of them, the territorial integrity, political independence or security of any of the Parties is threatened."

99. Morrison *supra* note 97.

100. Ibid.

101. "Rome Declaration on Peace and Cooperation," November 8, 1991, reprinted *NATO Review* (December 1991), 19.

102. The NATO foreign ministers agreed to cooperate with the Conference on Security and Cooperation in Europe (CSCE) in peacekeeping operations, asserting that

> we are prepared to support, on a case-by-case basis in accordance with our own procedures, peacekeeping activities under the responsibility of the CSCE, including by making available Alliance resources and expertise.

Para. 11, Final Communique of the Ministerial Meeting of the North Atlantic Council in Oslo on June 4, 1992, reprinted in *NATO Review* (June 1992), 31. At the December, 1992, Ministerial Meeting of the North Atlantic Council, the United Nations was added to the CSCE as a possible initiator of peacekeeping missions with which NATO may become involved. John Kriendler, "NATO's Changing Role: Opportunities and Constraints for Peacekeeping," *NATO Review* (August 1993).

103. Ibid. Kriendler notes the organizations limitations: "NATO is not prepared to undertake a peacekeeping operation on its own initiative; it is unlikely that such an approach would find a consensus among the Allies."

104. Recent settlement proposals have resulted from initiatives by the United Nations and the CSCE which did not require a separate NATO policy.

105. Kriendler, *supra* note 102.

106. See John Pomfret, "Serbs Withdrawn From Sarajevo Peaks," *Washington Post* (August 15, 1993). For the NATO actions, see Press Statement by the Secretary General following the Special Meeting of the North Atlantic Council in Brussels on August 2, 1993; Press Release (93) 52, Decisions taken at the Meeting of the North Atlantic Council on August 9, 1993.

107. The Deputy Secretary General of NATO has recently stated:

> The Alliance elaborated at its Rome Summit a conceptual basis for closer interaction with other security organizations. It is essential that we work in close cooperation and coordination with the United Nations, the CSCE, and the WEU. We need a highly integrated approach of all the security institutions in dealing with real and potential conflicts in Europe that permits and indeed encourages them to act simultaneously.

NATO Deputy Secretary General Amedeo de Franchis Address to an Atlantic Council of the United States 1993 Eurogroup Washington Conference, *Reuters Transcript Report* (May 5, 1993).

108. See Brian Urquhart, *A Life in Peace and War* (1987), 132-35.

109. Robert C. Riggs and Jack C. Plano, *The United Nations: International Organization and World Politics* (1988), 231-32.

110. See Edwin M. Smith, "NATO and the European Community: Troubled Transitions," *USC LAW* (Fall 1992), 2-11.

111. For example, while military units from NATO member states were heavily involved in the Gulf conflict, NATO's formal role was limited to

small deployments to assist in the territorial defense of Turkey, a NATO member which bordered upon Iraq. (It should be noted that NATO logistics facilities played a critical role in getting coalition forces to the Gulf.)

112. Alan W. Watts, *The Wisdom of Insecurity* (1951).

The United Nations in the Aftermath of Somalia: The Effects of the UN's Handling of Article 2(7) on the United Nations

Michael G. Schechter*

Nothing contained in the present Charter shall authorize the United Nations to intervene in matters which are essentially within the domestic jurisdiction of any state or shall require the Members to submit such matters to settlement under the present Charter; but this principle shall not prejudice the application of enforcement under Chapter VII."

Article 2(7) of the UN Charter

. . . in light of the domestic jurisdiction limitation of the Charter, it must be assumed that the [Security] Council would not authorize the Secretary-General to intervene with armed troops in an internal conflict when the Council has not specifically adopted enforcement measures under Article 41 and 42 of Chapter VII.

Dag Hammarskjold
August 21, 1960

*Professor of International Relations, Michigan State University. Appreciation is expressed to Thomas Ilgen of Pitzer College and W. Andy Knight of York University for their insightful comments on an earlier version of this chapter and to Chae-Jin Lee of Claremont McKenna College for organizing the conference at which an earlier version of this chapter was first presented.

At this critical stage [in world affairs], the mandatory principle of non-intervention by States in one another's internal affairs acquires added importance. Prudence and restraint will need to be fully employed to prevent internal upheavals in any state from becoming the cause of international conflicts.

Javier Pérez de Cuéllar
September 12, 1989

We need not impale ourselves on the horns of a dilemma between respect for sovereignty and the protection of human rights. The last thing the United Nations needs is a new ideological controversy. What is involved is not the right of intervention but the collective obligation of States to bring relief and redress in human rights emergencies.

Javier Pérez de Cuéllar
September 13, 1991

Violation of state sovereignty is and will remain, an offense against the global order. But its misuse may also undermine human rights and jeopardize a peaceful global life. Civil wars are no longer civil and the carnage they inflict will not let the world remain indifferent.

Boutros Boutros-Ghali
January 31, 1992

The time of absolute and exclusive sovereignty . . . has passed; its theory was never matched by reality. It is the task of leaders of States today to understand this and to find a balance between the needs of good internal governance and the requirements of an ever more interdependent world.

Boutros Boutros-Ghali
June 17, 1992

The purpose of this paper is to examine the evolution and consequences for the United Nations[1] of that organization's treatment of the slippery and contentious concept of state sovereignty.[2] The need for such an investigation seems obvious. There have long been those who have contended that the notion of "state sovereignty" is anachronistic[3] and biased, and even that for "all practical purposes" the UN has largely acted as if Article 2(7) did not exist.[4] But few have investigated the consequences for the UN of taking such a position.[5] Moreover, some things have clearly changed recently which also call for an analysis such as this one. The actions of the UN Security Council, especially in Iraq and Somalia but also in Haiti, Cambodia and what was once Yugoslavia, and the statements of recent Secretaries-General are something new.[6] As one careful observer and former UN secretariat official recently put it:

> The [Security] Council has long taken the position that intrastate conflict can threaten international security—as, for example, in Cyprus, southern Lebanon, Nicaragua, and, most recently, Yugoslavia. But the issue of UN "intervention"—a word still largely avoided[7]—to resolve or alleviate internal conflict and restore stability has not been posed so clearly or insistently as is the case now and is likely to be in the future.[8]

With the end of the Cold War, the Security Council "has become more assertive in its own right and the great powers have begun to rely on it more readily to initiate, legitimize and, in some cases, carry out intervention." Indeed, there seems to be a shift in the balance towards the right to intervene to protect human rights.

> The rule against external influence—meddling by busy-bodies in what was previously the private business of a state no longer applies when that business impacts on the conscience, the security and perhaps even the environment of the rest of the world. . . . The balance in favor of a "right to intervene," certainly as far as human rights are concerned, has shifted because in the post-Cold War era, security considerations are no longer paramount. Governments are now less inclined to ignore violations of human rights for the sake, for example, of the unity of the anti-Soviet alliance.[9]

Marks makes a related observation, pointing toward structural factors as the causal agents of change:

The disintegration of the Soviet Union and increasingly of Yugoslavia has forced to the forefront an issue that the Cold War kept under wraps for decades: the contradiction between the principle of self-determination of peoples, enshrined in Article 1 of the UN Charter and that of the political and territorial integrity of sovereign states, with an equally strong pedigree in the UN's fundamental law. [10]

Observing similar phenomena, former Secretary-General Pérez de Cuéllar (on April 24, 1991), pointed to subsystemic causes rather than structural ones:

We are witnessing what is probably an irreversible shift in public attitudes towards the belief that the defence of the oppressed in the name of morality should prevail over frontiers and legal documents. [11]

Whether the causal agents are structural or subsystemic or (more likely) some combination, it almost appears as if we are now witnessing the emergence and recognition of a legitimate *right* to intervene in the domestic affairs of member states in the name of community norms, values, or interests. [12] To date, there has been next to nothing written about the consequences of these most recent, seemingly quite new and remarkable statements and actions for the United Nations in the post-Cold War era. That is the purpose of this paper.

This study begins with an overview of the history of the concepts of state sovereignty and domestic jurisdiction as they relate to the United Nations. This section recounts the debates among international legal scholars about the meaning (or meaninglessness) of Article 2(7) as well as the way the related concepts of state sovereignty and domestic jurisdiction have been shaped (i.e., eroded) by UN debates and actions. [13] Particular attention is devoted to the Congo crisis where, in a significantly different international system, the Secretary General articulated a broad (some would say too broad) understanding of the *restraints* on UN action imposed by state sovereignty, with dire, almost fatal, consequences for the institution. Hammarskjold, keenly aware of the Soviet Union's opposition to an assertive, interventionist UN (especially one seemingly doing the "West's" bidding) chose to speak of restraints on the UN, precisely in a situation when such restraints seemed impossible on the ground.

Then attention is devoted to the likely consequences for the UN in the post-Cold War era, where the Permanent Five of the Security Council can be expected to reach consensus more frequently and where the Secretary-General is less inhibited in making bold statements and taking bold initiatives. Stated otherwise, what are the likely consequences for the UN, in the most current Secretary-General's words and the Security Council's actions, the position that the time of "absolute and exclusive sovereignty . . . has passed."[14] Information is provided to respond to questions such as the following. What does this imply for an organization whose chief membership criterion, indeed whose "fundamental principle," is state sovereignty?[15] What does this imply for support for the organization by members whose major foreign policy tools have included assertions of the rights of sovereign states,[16] especially in the post-Cold War[17] and at a time when funds for economic development are being squeezed out by collective security concerns? What does this imply for the future role of the UN and the organizational structure of the UN, especially in light of recent systemic changes? What are the consequences for the UN of only serving or at least being perceived as only capable of serving as an agent for change in the direction desired by the major powers?[18] Or, as Lyons and Mastanduno put it: what does this imply for restructuring a Security Council which has come to be criticized by some developing countries as "simply a vehicle for expressing and authorizing the collective intention of the great powers?"[19] What does this imply for the UN's claim to be the world's collective legitimizer, i.e., the institution capable of making and carrying out political decisions in accordance with universally accepted procedures and connected with universally accepted norms of behavior?[20]

The United Nations Charter, Legal Scholarly Debate and the Concept of Sovereignty

Discussion of the UN Charter, sovereignty and its related principles usually begins with a textual analysis and often a comparison with the League of Nations' experiences from which it evolved. The essential content of Article 2(7) of the

Charter is consistent with that of the League Covenant's Article 15(8) on which it is based:[21]

> If the dispute between the parties is claimed by one of them, and is found by the Council to arise out of a matter which by international law is solely within the domestic jurisdiction of that party, the Council shall so report, and shall make no recommendation as to its settlement.

But there are a few noteworthy changes. For example, Article 15 (8) excluded the League Council from having jurisdiction in a dispute which arose out of a matter solely within the domestic jurisdiction of a party to the dispute. The paradox of this provision was that an international body was charged with deciding whether an issue was solely within the domestic jurisdiction of the parties; in the process of that determination, of course, the issue was being handled by a body outside the states party to the dispute. The same paradox that had confronted the League could also apply to the United Nations. How could the UN discuss and investigate a matter to see if it is prohibited by Article 2(7) if the discussion and investigation itself was a sort of intervention into the affairs of member countries? However, the textual paradox in the UN's case is a bit more complicated. Unlike the Covenant provision, the Charter does not explicitly charge the UN, much less any particular UN organ, with deciding whether the issue is within a state's domestic jurisdiction.[22] Presumably such a determination could be made by one or more parties to the dispute–keeping in mind the "basic and proper principle of international law that no state can be judge in its own cause"[23]–a situation unlikely to readily resolve the dilemma in many instances, and apparently not really what the members had in mind.[24] In addition, the omission of the phrase *under international law* allows for a political interpretation rather than a legal one.[25] In practice, the UN's political organs have not shown any disposition to have jurisdictional questions related to Article 2(7) adjudicated by the International Court of Justice, in spite of the fact that members have called for it from time to time.[26]

Also unlike the League Covenant, Article 2(7) of the Charter does not explicitly refer to disputes and it prohibits not only recommendations of the Council but any kind of intervention by *any* organ of the United Nations (except for the Chapter VII exception). This seems particularly problematic in light of the use of the ambiguous verb intervene and the charge to the UN under Chapters IX and X and especially Articles 55 and 56. Article 55 authorizes the UN to promote higher standards of living and work to solve problems of economic, social, health and related problems. Article 56 calls upon member states to "take joint and separate action in cooperation with the Organization for the achievement of the purposes set forth in Article 55." This latter article might be interpreted to mean that member states are obligated to permit the UN to intervene even if the matters are essentially within their domestic jurisdiction. Kelsen concludes that "this provision is hardly consistent with Article 2, paragraph 7,"[27] in part presumably, because he also contended that there was no real import to the change in terminology from the League's wording of solely to the UN's essentially within. He conceded, however, that there would be significant consequences if his view were not sustained.[28]

On the other hand, it would be wrong to assume that those writing the Charter were completely unaware of these dilemmas and seeming inconsistencies. For example, at the 17th meeting of the UN Conference on International Organization, the United States delegate made clear that broadening the UN's functions—relative to those of the League or even the original Dumbarton Oaks' proposals—to include enabling the UN to eradicate the underlying causes of war, required broadening of the exclusionary concept relating to domestic jurisdiction.[29] Moreover, during the Congressional hearings relating to the UN, State Department representatives seemed to concede that ". . . the principle of non-intervention in domestic affairs—however this concept may be defined—is hardly compatible with the functions the Charter confers upon the Organization in Chapters IX and X."[30]

This brief analysis evidences the *intended* ambiguities in the language of Article 2(7) and the early recognition that it conflicted with other UN priorities articulated in the Charter. Moreover, such an overview reveals the problematic process provided for in the Charter for resolving controversies over those ambiguities, leaving it open to member states and various UN organs to argue and to shape the concept through practice.

Such a development seems wholly compatible, if not inevitable, in light of the Permanent Court of Justice's opinion that ". . . [the] question of whether the jurisdiction of a State is essentially a relative question; it depends upon the development of international relations."[31]

The United Nations In Practice and the Concept of Sovereignty

Given this situation, it is not surprising that the UN wrestled with this issue almost immediately. At the first joint meeting of the First and Sixth Committees of the General Assembly (November 21, 1946), the South African delegate, Field-Marshal Smuts, contended that a UN General Assembly *recommendation* relating to the treatment of Indians in the Union of South Africa would be <u>intervention</u> in a matter <u>essentially</u> within the domestic jurisdiction of his sovereign state. On the other hand, he did not express any objection to the issue being freely discussed, which it was.[32] And perhaps more interestingly, he felt that an <u>exception</u> to the rule of domestic jurisdiction "might be sought in the direction of human rights and fundamental freedoms, such as the right to exist, the right to freedom of conscience and freedom of speech, and the right of free access to the courts." However, he contended that none of those applied in this instance, nor for that matter was there yet

> . . . any internationally recognized formulation of such rights, and the Charter itself did not define them. Member States, therefore, did not have any specific obligations under the Charter, whatever other moral obligations might rest upon them.[33]

As a follow-up to that discussion, the General Assembly adopted a resolution at its 52nd plenary meeting (December 8, 1946) which was a statement of fact, the expression of opinion and the request to report. But it did not contain a recommendation nor did it formally decide the question of whether the matter was essentially within the domestic jurisdiction of a member state.[34]

The "first clear interference in domestic internal affairs" by the UN is often taken to be the General Assembly's examination of Spain's form of government.[35] This was also in December 1946. The General Assembly passed a resolution which recommended banning Spain from the UN and its Specialized Agencies and requested that all member states recall their ambassadors from Spain. "It also stated that if a democratic Spanish government was not established within a reasonable time, the Security Council should consider adequate measures to remedy the situation."[36] There is no question that, in this instance at least, "extra legal factors" led to the idea ". . . that matters *prima facie* of domestic jurisdiction may be of international concern in certain circumstances."[37]

A similar conclusion could be reached about the General Assembly's position that non self-governing territories were outside the limitation contained in Article 2(7), in spite of objections by the colonial powers.[38] The Assembly's disregard of "domestic jurisdiction" as it relates to issues of self-determination was seen to flow logically from its treatment of non self-governing territories more generally and because of a belief that it was problem that if not resolved, it would inevitably affect the maintenance of international peace and security. Over time, the General Assembly virtually established the principle that the denial of the right of self-determination is ". . . a matter of international concern and so no longer within the sovereign domain of a State."[39]

More generally, the Assembly has come to largely disregard Article 2(7) on issues "of human rights and fundamental freedoms," presumably in line with the aforementioned position taken by Smut, or at least to focus on other articles of the Charter which were also intimately connected to the Charter's preamble [(including 1(3), 13(2), and 76(c)]. This was evident, for example, in criticism of the former Eastern bloc. At its third annual session in 1949, the Assembly adopted a resolution expressing concern at the "grave accusations made against the governments of Bulgaria and Hungary regarding the suppression of human rights and fundamental freedoms." At the same session, the Soviet Union was called upon to change its policies which prevented wives of foreign nationals from leaving their own country to join their husbands, a topic of considerable prior discussion in the Sixth Committee of the General Assembly (December 2-7, 1948).[40]

At least at the outset, when the General Assembly began to discuss particularly sensitive "domestic" economic and social issues, it couched its language carefully. For example, the Assembly's first recommendations in the area of population growth went out of their way to recognize "the sovereignty of nations" in formulating and promoting their population policies, offering UN assistance and advice only at the request of member states. Subsequently, however, the General Assembly passed resolutions, for example, contending that the World Population Plan of Act

> is an instrument of the international community for the promotion of economic development, quality of life, human rights and fundamental freedoms within the broader context of the internationally adopted strategies for national and international progress.[41]

Thus the trend in General Assembly recommendations appears linear. First in the area of human rights and fundamental freedoms, subsequently in economic and social fields more generally, and finally in the area of international peace and security, the General Assembly—meaning the majority of the member states—overcame whatever inhibitions state sovereignty had once presented to it in the area of recommendations.[42]

The Security Council and the Secretary-General, however, were much more inhibited, not least of all because they had different political constituencies, significantly different powers (i.e., being more than mere recommendations), and—in the case of the Security Council—the added burden of the veto.[43] The care with which the Secretary-General has dealt with the issue of state sovereignty was, of course, underscored by U Thant's adherence to Nasser's request that he remove the UNEF I troops from what became the eve of the Six Days War and especially Hammarskjold in the Congo crisis.[44] A few more extended comments about the Congo crisis are warranted for it raised three decades ago some of the same legal questions now being debated. It also, of course, arose in the Cold War and had the most dire of consequences for the UN itself: initially the Soviet call for Hammarskjold's replacement by a *troika*, generally expected to seriously undermine the institution's power and autonomy, and ultimately Hammarskjold's death.

The Congo crisis led to arguments over the second aspect of Article 2(7), i.e., the exception for Chapter VII activities. The debate focused on whether the exception to intervening in a sovereign state's domestic jurisdiction applied to *all* Chapter VII measures (i.e., provisional and coercive, hortatory and decisional) or merely military enforcement measures; whether it applied only to enforcement measures taken under Article 42[45] or whether it applied to actions taken under any part of the Chapter.[46] Further questions were raised as to whether the exception was limited to enforcement measures taken by the UN against states or whether it might include measures taken against other entities which endangers international peace but requires intervention in a state's domestic domains (e.g., helping a regime quell a rebellion, insurrection, a guerilla campaign or a secessionist movement).[47]

The legal debate was further complicated by the fact that, from the outset, Hammarskjold took the position that the Security Council had not permitted intervention in the domestic jurisdiction of the Congo because it had not explicitly authorized the Congo operation under Article 41 or 42, which presumably he believed would be necessary for the exceptions to Article 2(7) to apply. Further, while the ICJ, in the *United Nations Expenses Case*, did not explicitly address the issue of Article 2(7), it shared with Hammarskjold the view that the operations did not involve action "against a State" and therefore, presumably, were not based on Article 42. All of this contributed to the argument that the UN, as the crisis progressed, had indeed interfered in the internal affairs of a member state, presumably in contradiction of its own Charter. Such an argument, of course, strengthened the Soviets' hand in attacking Hammarskjold. But, as Gross eloquently argues, none of this is necessarily relevant to the legal issues at hand. Gross contends that the Article 2(7) exception was intended to apply to all Chapter VII operations, and thus was not limited to enforcement measures against states. He explains away the ICJ's holding by the fact that it was made early on in the Congo crisis. Gross' position, of course, obviates any concern with the fact that the Security Council was vague about the specific Chapter VII articles under which it was authorizing action in the Congo, a situation he finds typical and explainable by political rather than legal factors. More importantly for our purposes, such an interpretation suggests that the Secretary-General overstated the limitations on his actions owing to Article 2(7), possibly for political reasons, that is, to avoid confrontation with the Soviets and possible Soviet vetoes over the UN's actions. In so doing, however, he set himself and the organization up for unwarranted criticism, a lesson seemingly not lost on his successors nor on the Security Council's "Permanent Five" who authored subsequent "interventionist" resolutions.

The United Nations in the Post-Cold War Era

Election Monitoring in Haiti

Requests for the UN to monitor elections are not novel. Secretaries-General have long received and usually rejected such requests, in part because of the touchiness of the sovereignty/domestic jurisdiction issue.[48]   On the other hand, the UN has long been involved in monitoring plebiscites, including in instances of decolonization and in elections in areas of regional conflict.[49]   The UN's involvement there is often part and parcel of the peace accord.[50]   What was novel about Haiti was that it represented the first time that the United Nations agreed to monitor an election "in an independent nation not involved in a regional conflict."[51]   What is most important for our analysis here, however, relates to: (1) the role of the Secretary-General, who was strongly supportive of this precedent; (2) the opposition of several Latin American countries, led by Mexico;[52] (3) the role of the Security Council, under U.S. leadership, and (4) the possible implications of this precedent, including those articulated by Franck, Schachter and Russett.

The initial request for UN assistance came from Interim Haitian President Ertha Parcal. The Secretary-General's immediate response was to deploy a fact-finding mission at the end of March 1991. On it, he included Horacio Braneo, the Deputy Head of the UN Observer Mission for the Verification of Elections in Nicaragua. At the conclusion of the mission, the Secretary-General's spokesperson noted that the two-week mission had been "of a technical nature."[53]   The care with which that statement was crafted may have had something to do with the "third world" opposition, led by Mexico, to any UN electoral role in Haiti:[54] even if the language of the press release did not, the more than four month delay in responding to the Haitian government's request clearly did. The core of Mexico's opposition is evident in the statement made by the head of its delegation to the General Assembly, Olga Pellicer, at the time that she (finally and reluctantly) endorsed the resolution for holding elections with an international presence:

> The Mexican delegation understands that sending this mission will not set a precedent in respect of the domestic jurisdiction of States. My delegation wishes to restate its unshakable conviction that the electoral processes lie within the domain in which domestic legislation in each State is sovereign. The United Nations mission is being sent in this case only because it was requested by Haiti.[55]

With a view toward past history of hegemonic intervention, the "third world's" opposition, as presented most prominently by Mexico,[56] was to avoid going down the slippery slope of lost state sovereignty. They seem to fear precisely what Franck welcomes. In discussing "democracy as the ultimate global entitlement," one presumably almost universally shared in the post-1989 world, Franck notes that

> while the notion of political participation appears to be a radical departure from strict views of state equality, which have tended to emphasize equal sovereignty and noninterference in all nations' domestic affairs, there has long been a trend toward a global conscience capable of interfering where injustice reigns. . . . What is new is the idea that the system should include among those gross abuses the denial of a population's right to participate democratically in the process of governance.

Franck portrays such an evolution as simply bringing the notion of self-determination into the 21st century.[57] Holmes' vision is similar, but his explanation differs a bit:

> As the United Nations [in the post-Cold War era] adopts the principles of global democracy and redefines the notion of state sovereignty, LDCs' ability to restrict

international interference will be diminished. The new thinking is that the if all U.N. member-states are equal voices in a global democratic order, then LDCs not only have a right to interfere in the internal affairs of other states through the United Nations, but can expect to have their independence restricted as well by that organization.[58]

Perceptively, Franck went on to suggest that the slope does not necessarily end there, noting the need eventually to confront the "murkier realm of systemic enforcement" (e.g., what is to be done when there is a negative finding on compliance after an election; a party being exposed before its own people).[59]   In this regard, he notes the possibility of withdrawing full rights (of state equality) from such states, as has been done in the past for "pariah" states or the imposition of economic sanctions, as was done with Rhodesia in the aftermath of the U.D.I.[60]

Significantly, in introducing the draft resolution on election monitoring in Haiti, the Bolivian delegate (speaking on behalf of the Bahamas, Belize, Colombia, Ecuador, El Salvador, Jamaica, Haiti, Peru and Venezuela) had underscored that the assistance being provided ". . . does not have and should not have any connections with questions of international peace and security."[61]   This was an interesting preambular passage, presumably alluding to the fact that before its final passage in the General Assembly, the proposal had been referred by the Secretary-General to the Security Council,[62] where, with enthusiastic support from the U.S. and France, it had been warmly endorsed.[63]

Thus the Haitian case is additionally significant because of the roles which the U.S. and UN Secretary-General played in siding with that group of "third world" countries which were less concerned with maintaining whatever purity was left in the notion of sovereignty[64] and the "domestic jurisdiction" clause.[65]   Hypotheses to explain these strange bedfellows are easy to come by.   The Haitians, like the Namibians and Nicaraguans before them, were firmly convinced of the collective legitimization value of having the UN (even more than regional organizations, much less unofficial observers) monitor elections, especially given the relatively minimal costs for doing so (i.e., the United Nations underscored that it was acceding to Haiti's request).   The UN Secretary-General's pro-active role in this regard was facilitated by the post-Cold War Security Council consensus. It might also be explained in terms of the Secretary-General's moral commitment to expanding democratization in Latin America or in terms of simple bureaucratic factors.

While the immediate future seems to include election monitoring in situations more akin to those in the past than in the Haitian case—for example, in Cambodia, Afghanistan and the Western Sahara—there are those who urge the UN Secretary-General to build extensively on the Haitian experience. There are also those who raise questions about where the Security Council, under U.S. leadership, might be heading in this issue area and, we could add, what the consequences of that might be for UN.

Not surprisingly, among the most notable urging the Secretary-General to follow up on the Haitian experience is Franck himself:

First the United Nations must recognize a defined normative right [of democratic governance and to enjoy freedom from totalitarian oppression]. Then there must be a credible process for monitoring compliance with this right. Finally, in response to violations, the international community must exert degrees of nonviolent pressure, such as the deprivation of the privileges that the community bestows on legitimate governments.[66]

Schachter wonders where all of this is eventually heading: "A basic question is whether the Security Council may determine the structure of government (e.g., unity or federalism) and even select the rulers (e.g., replace a ruler guilty of aggression) in order to secure international peace."[67] Russett's thinking is along the same lines:

. . . it is imaginable that UN monitoring of elections and certification of these elections as free, democratic, and legitimate may be made conditional on agreement among the parties that the UN retains the right, for a limited time, to intervene militarily if necessary to protect any government brought to power. . . .[68]

While Franck's, Schachter's and Russett's propositions may sound a bit far fetched, and certainly would have during the Cold War, they sound a bit less so in the aftermath of recent global structural changes and related UN actions.[69] The full import of Franck's, Russett's, and Schachter's propositions can only be envisioned when one realizes that the Security Council's actions seem virtually impossible to overrule, a point made most vivid in its recent actions relating to sanctions on Libya for not returning Westerners to be tried outside of Libya.[70]

UN Intervention in Iraq

Although a very complex case, the discussion of the Iraqi case can be relatively brief because of its familiarity. The most important consequences for the UN coming out of the Iraqi case have as much to do with the statements of the UN Secretary-General, and the way President Bush was seen to *use* the UN Security Council, as the actions themselves. The biggest controversy in the U.S. international legal community seemed to focus on the absence of any specific Charter articles being cited in the key Security Council resolutions, an issue discussed earlier in the context of the Congo crisis.[71] More relevant for our purposes is the role of the UN Secretary-General in these events and the possible precedents relating to intervention for human rights reasons and to compel compliance with arms control agreements.[72] Even here, the legal precedents are relatively insignificant. As more than one observer has pointed out: victors in war have never been inhibited by concerns with state sovereignty in imposing their will on those who have surrendered.[73] What is essential for the future of the UN, however, is the perception, especially of "third world" countries,[74] of the UN in relation to state sovereignty,[75] that emerged from the Persian Gulf War.[76] This perception was of the same nature as that in the Haitian case but much, much more dramatic.

The Iraqi case, however, is one where the Secretary-General appears to have been quite concerned about the possible consequences for the UN, presumably because of the differences in the nature of the UN's activities (military intervention as contrasted to election monitoring) and the nature of the opposition to what the Security Council was now warmly endorsing. Pérez de Cuéllar's ambivalence was not limited to the Security Council's resolutions, which, in his negotiations with Saddam Hussein, he was willing to have described as U.S. and not UN resolutions.   Rather he kept a low profile throughout the crisis.   He did not comment on the Security Council resolutions and he was conspicuously absent when the vote was taken to enforce the embargo.[77]   He disliked the deadlines imposed, joined forces with the French and Soviets in contending that the U.S. needed a Security Council resolution in order to bring about a blockade, and he was fearful that his meeting with Saddam Hussein—which he (rightfully) expected to be unsuccessful—could be used as a trigger to military action.[78] It was his idea that the rightful UN role would be to provide a peace-keeping force to monitor and police an Iraqi withdrawal from Kuwait, a position which had no chance to prevail given Iraqi intransigence.

One consequence of the Iraqi defeat was the outbreak of a Kurdish revolt in Northern Iraq.   The Iraqi army's suppression of the revolt led up to 2,000,000 Kurds to flee into the mountains.   Thereupon, Allied troops occupied northern Iraq in order to provide food, shelter and medical aid for the refugees and to keep the Iraqi military from advancing further.   In supporting the Allied initiative, some Western European countries seemed to be endorsing "the most radical argument" for disregarding national sovereignty, one which holds that a request from those who are suffering is sufficient to justify crossing a boundary without authorization from a country's leaders.   The humanitarian imperative takes precedence over non-interference with a state's sovereignty.[79]   As former U.S. Ambassador to the U.N. Thomas Pickering put it:

> While the world has seen the sovereign exercise of butchery before, this is the first time that a significant number of governments have rejected a state's right to do so and acted using military forces to prevent it by providing humanitarian assistance and protection directly to the victims.[80]

Throughout, however, the Allies were calling for UN humanitarian intervention to eliminate the perception that they were acting "unilaterally."   But the UN Secretary-General was keenly aware of the implications of doing so.

The Secretary-General was most reluctant to accept the challenge, even though some members of his staff urged him to do so in order to be able to invoke humanitarian intervention as a justification for disregarding the Charter's strictures against intervening in the domestic affairs of member states. Pérez de Cuéllar pointed to the absence of authorization by any major UN organ, denial of access by Iraq, lack of clarity about what the mandate of a UN force ought to be, the reluctance of China and the Soviet Union (neither wanted to create a precedent for such an excuse), and the active opposition of many Third World countries.[81]

Gardner explains the alluded lack of a Security Council mandate relating to the collective right to intervene for exclusively human rights purposes this way:

Had such a claim been made on human rights grounds, the resolution would most certainly have been vetoed by China, and possibly by the Soviet Union; it would almost definitely have drawn the negative votes of India and some of the Latin American and African countries among the Council's non-permanent members.[82]

Instead, in Resolution 688 (relating to Northern Iraq), the Security Council chose to live with the tensions between two fundamental Charter principles. It upheld both sovereign inviolability and the need to defend human welfare. In it the Security Council chose not to redefine either, nor to argue that the protection of human rights was not a violation of sovereignty. Instead, they linked human rights with international peace and security: failure to protect the Kurds would threaten the security of sovereignty of neighboring countries, which in turn would threaten Iraq further. This was not intended to set any legal precedents.[83]

Still the Resolution was not without controversy. Some portrayed it as precedent setting in the sense that it authorized military intervention without securing the consent of the Iraqi government. To some this signalled a change in international norms and reflected the expansion of the authority of the international community in the aftermath of the Cold War.[84] It certainly differed from the aforementioned Congo case in this regard.

Minear and Weiss indicated a more subtle cause for long-term concern on the part of the UN, coming out of the same set of events.

> The association of humanitarian action with political-military strategy also affected the perception of the United Nations among governments and aid agencies. Government officials in Jordan and Iran noted the extent to which aid from the world organization closely mirrored the political-military objectives of the allied coalition. Had Turkey incurred the expenditures on evacuees for which Jordan is being denied reimbursement, said the Jordanians the funds would have been provided with the stroke of a pen. . . . We got the refugees, said the Iranians, but Turkey got the funds. For its part, the Iraqi government saw the concentration of U.N. efforts on the Kurds—also the focus of political-military strategy of the allied coalition—as discrediting the United Nations' avowed humanitarian objectives. The Iraqis felt that U.N. assistance should have been oriented toward needs throughout Iraq.[85]

Not surprisingly then, the UN has found considerable "hostility" toward its humanitarian efforts.[86] Thus its activities in one priority area have partly undermined those in another.[87]

The actions of the General Assembly in the Iraqi case were a bit more dramatic, but no less ambiguous than those of the Security Council:

> The UN General Assembly, always given to hyperbole, responded by announcing the creation of a 'new international humanitarian order.' Yet the content of that 'order' remains elusive. On the one hand, the Assembly held that in the event of emergencies, "the principles of humanity, neutrality and impartiality must be given utmost consideration by all those involved in providing humanitarian assistance"; but on the other hand, it emphasized "the sovereignty of affected States and their primary role in the initiation, organization, coordination and implementation of humanitarian assistance within their respective territories."

Haas concludes that "We are long way from a consensus on the primacy of a right to intervene on behalf of refugees, starving people, or democracy."[88]

Thus while the Iraqi case presents relatively few clear legal precedents, it obviously had long-term consequences for the UN, particularly in its relations with those most disturbed by the degree to which the UN appeared to be ignoring some "third world" states' sovereign boundaries and by the way in which the U.S. and its allies appeared to be able to use the UN, especially the Security Council, but also a relatively reluctant Secretary-General, for their own purposes.[89]

Humanitarian Intervention: Somalia, Yugoslavia and Cambodia

The Somalian, Yugoslav and Cambodian cases shall be discussed even more briefly because of their familiarity and because they are on-going. But here the precedents appear clearer and the long-term consequences for the UN likely to be even more pervasive.

Unlike in the case of Iraq, the Secretary-General took a leadership role in the Somalian case at the same time that he tried to distance himself from the U.S., indeed—at times—to make it appear as if the UN were using, or at least outsmarting, the U.S. rather than vice versa. The new Secretary-General chided its members, especially the United States, into intervening rather than focusing all of their attention on the less (in total human numbers) devastating crisis in the former state of Yugoslavia, a crisis where Security Council unanimity proved much more difficult to achieve in any event. The Somalian case is most noteworthy because: (1) the justification given was clearly understood to be humanitarian intervention, although it was again stated in terms of a threat to international peace and security;[90] (2) the intervention was done with the world's acquiescence even though there was no invitation from what anyone could contend was a *de facto* or *de jure* government of Somalia, and (3) the plan, from the outset, was to begin with U.S. troops which would eventually be withdrawn in order to turn the operations over to a UN force.

The Yugoslav and Somalian cases differ substantially in detail from events in Cambodia, but all share a number of essential characteristics, at least for the purposes of this analysis. All three arose in the aftermath of Cold War, something seemingly essential to the pro-active actions and statements which came to characterize the Security Council and Secretary-General. In all three situations, it is hard to argue that there was an authoritative government whose sovereignty was being transgressed. All three are civil war situations. And, as seen in the Congo three decades earlier, this often leads the UN to perform administrative tasks, including those normally fulfilled by a sovereign government. In the case of Cambodia, this is inextricably tied to UNCTAC's (the United Nations Transitional Authority for Cambodia) charge. In cooperation with almost all other agencies in the UN system, it is to organize and conduct elections that will determine the composition of the government of a post-civil war Cambodia.

> The UN is also to reintroduce a normal life for Cambodians. Because of the centrality of the election as a way of permanently reconciling the four contending factions, the UN has the power to second-guess all government agencies involved, supervising the police, the courts, and the ministry of the interior. Other units will repatriate and resettle up to 400,000 civilian refugees. Military units will monitor the cease-fire; disarm, regroup, and house the guerrillas; and prevent the reintroduction of imported arms.[91]

Such a charge could almost equally well apply to Somalia, although probably not in the former Yugoslavia.

Taken by themselves, these are not precedent-setting in any very dramatic way. It is easy—as many have contended—to argue away the relevance of Article 2(7) and questions of state sovereignty and domestic jurisdiction when there are no authoritative governments in place. On the other hand, it can be countered that the dichotomy between authoritative governments, which merit the rights of sovereign states, and those which are not, is much less a dichotomy than a continuum, as so well articulated in Jackson's book on "quasi-sovereign" states.[92] Further, it is relatively easy to portray these on-going crises as simply the logical culmination of the erosion of Article 2(7) that began in Cold War days on the floors of the UN even before it moved into Turtle Bay, continued through the Congo and on into the post-Cold War era of the Iraqi crises where Secretaries-General resisted such erosion or at least took steps not to be identified as its proponents, through the Somalian case, where the Secretary-General took a leadership role. But to conclude this study, we need to go one step further . . . to begin to project the consequences *for the UN* of this trend, not yet complete, nor consistently linear, but more pointed in direction than was ever possible in a Cold War dominated environment.

Conclusions

The most obvious conclusion is that we have observed a significant erosion of protection afforded by Article 2(7), especially in the post-Cold War era. Or stated more positively, we have seen a significant expansion of the role of the international community at the expense of individual states.[93] The problem with such a statement, of course, is that we have also observed that much of that expansion has been seen as occurring under the guidance and sometimes with the push (as in Iraq) of the great powers, over the opposition of some "third world" states and with the acquiescence of others. To some extent this great power concert—which some see as implicit in a UN Charter which privileges the Security Council and within that body, privileges the Permanent Five—seems more evident now than ever before in the post-WWII era. The consequences of this seem to portend a weakening of the UN's claim to collective legitimization and universal respect.

The trend has not been totally linear, however, nor is it anywhere complete. While Hammarskjold's broad interpretation of Article 2(7) was not echoed by Pérez de Cuéllar during the Persian Gulf War, much less by Boutros-Boutros Ghali more recently, Pérez de Cuéllar's pro-active stance in regard to expanding international election monitoring contrasted dramatically with his reluctant role during the Persian Gulf crisis. Likewise, while the General Assembly, led by the "tyranny of its 'third world' majority," was quick to overcome objections to discussions and resolutions relating to *apartheid* and the rights of peoples in non-self governing territories, it has been much more conflicted on the right to intervene on behalf of refugees, starving people or democracy, much less to grant access to oil or other natural resources as if they were the common heritage of the world's peoples. And throughout the period surveyed, the Security Council has been most cautious in terms of the language it has used in expanding its powers relative to individual states' sovereignty.

But the cumulative effect of all of these trends—halting, non-linear, cautious as they be—is three-fold: (1) the meaningfulness of Article 2(7) as an element in any country's foreign policy arsenal is more limited than ever; (2) the Secretary-General himself has come to be viewed as one of the agents attacking the concept of state sovereignty and not one of those defending Article 2(7); and (3) the Security Council's attacks on state sovereignty have been blamed on the fact that it has become a captive of the major powers, especially the U.S., in the post-Cold War era. This is true in spite of the fact that, as the aforementioned survey suggests, in many instances it was some "third world" countries which took the leadership role, primarily but not exclusively in the General Assembly, in helping in the erosion of Article 2(7).

The consequences of these trends are as interesting as they are important. Any proposal to revise the UN's structure, if it emanates from "the North," is likely to be viewed by many of the UN's voting members with suspicion.[94] This is true, even if the goal is to further democratize the Security Council, to enhance the coordination of the UN's aid activities,[95] to expand the UN's early warning mechanisms including through the use of satellites, to expand the Organization's capacity for monitoring elections or supervising adherence to human rights conventions, much less to reword Article 2(7) in order to bring it into the 21st century or to allow non-state actors voting privileges in the General Assembly.

The perceived role of the UN Secretary-General and some of the UN's relief agencies as agents furthering the erosion of Article 2(7) may have even more direct long-term consequences. For it suggests that "third world" support of the Secretariat is likely to dissipate as well as their support of the Security Council. The only saving grace—for the UN, not for "third world" countries—is their lack of any obvious alternative to the UN for effectuating some of their foreign policy goals.

Consequently, reform of the United Nations is a necessary post-Cold War era priority if the UN is to be an authoritative agent of social and political change and an effective agent of collective legitimization. Such reform initiatives, however, can not be perceived as coming from the Secretariat, much less the Security Council, if they are to have a chance for passage. Moreover, such reforms, in order to restore the UN to its place as an effective tool in the foreign policy arsenals of most countries in the world, will have to go to the core of the UN's decision-making processes to include both formal and informal veto practices.

Notes to The United Nations in the Aftermath of Somalia

1. The focus of this chapter is on the major organs of the UN, although the theoretical issues which animate it are relevant to the Specialized and Related Agencies as well. In regard to the IMF, for example, Gold noted that the Fund's original Articles of Agreement ". . . represented a major departure from the principle of the past that each country was sovereign in the determination and management of the exchange rate of its currency." Joseph Gold, *Legal and Institutional Aspects of the International Monetary System, Selected Essays II* (Washington: International Monetary Fund, 1984), 240-41. See also, 570. One of the most balanced and sophisticated discussions of the Bank, Fund and UNDP in this regard remains Gordenker's. His statements are clear and persuasively documented:

> The reality of the second half of the twentieth century is that economic and social programs may have steadily eroded the margins of de facto domestic jurisdiction. Governments have progressively become involved in a process which tends to require conformity to implicit and explicit standards set in central institutions outside of their control. . . . It would be inaccurate, however, to suppose that this erosion of domestic jurisdiction has become the equivalent of control by international organizations.

Leon Gordenker, *International Aid and National Decisions: Development Programs in Malawi, Tanzania, and Zambia* (Princeton: Princeton University Press, 1976), 14.

2. "Strictly construed, sovereignty implies that states are subject only to constraints necessary to ensure the reciprocal rights of other states and to such rules as they freely accept as obligatory. . . . To be sure, these normative expressions of sovereignty are not wholly factual. Obviously states are not free from external influences in their conduct of affairs." Oscar Schachter, "Sovereignty and Threats to Peace," in *Collective Security in a Changing World*, edited by Thomas G. Weiss (Boulder: Lynne Rienner Publishers, 1993), 20.

3. Camilleri and Falk are among the most eloquent:

> The state continues to perform important economic, administrative and diplomatic functions, but these must not be confused with the exercise of sovereignty. Much of

contemporary social and political reality, whether reflected in the popular politics of movements and localities or economic interaction in the global domain, is not captured, much less explained, by the discourse of sovereignty. . . . The contemporary world is one where community, autonomy and the division between *internal* and *external* have become sharply contested categories, where the institutional foundations of sovereignty are themselves under challenge.

They explain this state of affairs by five phenomena: (1) internationalization of production, trade and finance; (2) homogenizing architecture of technological change; (3) globalization of the security dilemma; (4) escalating impact of ecological change; and (5) rise of local and transnational social consciousness. Joseph Camilleri and Jim Falk, *The End of Sovereignty? The Politics of a Shrinking and Fragmenting World* (Aldershot, England: Edward Elgar Publishing, Ltd., 1992), 242 and 246. For a similar argument, see: Mark W. Zacher, "The Decaying Pillars of the Westphalian Temple: Implications for International Order and Governance," in *Governance Without Government: Order and Change in World Politics*, Edited by James N. Rosenau and Ernst-Otto Czempiel (Cambridge: Cambridge University Press, 1992).

4. Writing in the early 1980s, Gross contended that UN actions, except for the Congo, would have been the same had Article 2(7) not existed and that many of the legal interpretations of Article 2(7) have sought to "emasculate" the article and, in so doing, run counter to a "canon of [legal] interpretation, namely, that 'an interpretation is not admissible which would make a provision meaningless, or ineffective.'" Leo Gross, *Essays on International Law and Organization*, Volume II (New York: Transnational Publishers, Inc., 1984), 1179 and 1180.

5. A somewhat related recent work is that by Kim R. Holmes. His intention is to dampen the "unrealistically elevated expectations" of some in the aftermath of the recent flurry of UN activities. While his article is useful—particularly in reminding readers of the mixed historical record of UN activities (especially those which Alan James has called "internal peacekeeping" in his more detailed study) and the potential costs, including the financial costs—of peacekeeping, peace-making and what Holmes chooses to call "warmaking," it does not draw the connections nor present the sort of analysis which this piece does. "A New World Disorder: A Critique of the United Nations," *Journal of International Affairs*, 46 (Winter 1993). Alan James, "Internal Peacekeeping: A Dead End for the UN?," paper presented

at the 1993 Annual Meetings of the International Studies Association, Alcapulco, March 1993.

6. As shall be shown later, there are precedents for almost all of the actions which the UN took, although the scope and frequency of the UN contributing to the erosion of Article 2(7) appear unprecedented. Klintworth traces precedents for intervening for human rights reasons, for example, back to the world community's outlawing of slavery centuries ago. Gary Klintworth, "'The Right to Intervene' in the Domestic Affairs of States," *Australian Journal of International Affairs*, 46 (November 1992), 248.

On the other hand, as the aforenoted quotes suggest, the language of the two most recent Secretaries-General signifies a significant shift. The importance of this is underscored by Walker's contention that the "story of state sovereignty" is said to celebrate a reading of history centered on the West, a story premised on a statist reading of history. Such a way of seeing the world, Walker suggests, has had significant consequences for defining problems beyond existing claims of sovereignty, as in the sea, outer space and the global commons more generally. But one need not be deconstructionist to accept that language has importance in the world (and institutions) of politics. R.B.J. Walker, "State Sovereignty and the Articulation of Political Space/Time," *Millennium: Journal of International Studies*, 20 (Winter 1991), 450-451 and 456. See also: R.B.J. Walker, *Inside/Outside: International Relations of Political Theory* (Cambridge: Cambridge University Press, 1993).

7. In part this may be explained by Anderson's observation that: "Until recently, international opinion has dismissed most prescriptions for UN sponsored intervention as immoral." He goes on to note that even in the post-UN intervention in Iraq era,

> . . . the United Nations has not codified conditions justifying intervention to prevent systematic state-sponsored human rights violations, or to prevent nuclear proliferation to hostile terrorist organizations.

James H. Anderson, "New World Order and State Sovereignty: Implications for UN-Sponsored Intervention," *The Fletcher Forum of World Affairs*, 16 (Summer 1992), 128 and 129.

8. Former Director of the Executive Office of the UN Secretary-General Sutterlin continued in a similar vein.

Nor did the Council, until the Gulf War, have to face the difficult question of whether it may (or, indeed, must) intervene if a government, through its actions, threatened the lives and basic human rights of a significant number of its population. . . . There are two other broad problems not foreseen when the mandate of the Security Council was defined that can patently threaten international security in a profound way [without necessarily involving formal actions outside a state's sovereign boundaries]: (1) willful and serious destruction of the global ecosystem and (2) the acquisition by a country, in contravention to treaty obligations, of nuclear weapons or other weapons of mass destruction that constitute a threat to global security.

Obviously the Iraqi crisis exemplifies both of these problems. James S. Sutterlin, "United Nations Decisionmaking: Future Initiatives for the Security Council and the Secretary-General," in *Collective Security in a Changing World*, edited by Thomas G. Weiss (Boulder: Lynne Rienner Publishers, 1993), 121-22.

9. Klintworth, "Right to Intervene," 248.

10. Stephen P. Marks, *The United Nations and Human Rights: New Challenges, New Responses*, The Ralph Bunche Institute on the United Nations, Occasional Papers Series, Number IX (New York: The Graduate School and University Center, The City University of New York, October 1991), 5.

11. As quoted in: Christopher Greenwood, "Is There a Right of Humanitarian Intervention?," *The World Today*, 49 (February, 1993), 35.
Anderson sees the 1975 Helsinki Accords as the crucial watershed in the shifting balance to which the Secretary-General alludes, for ". . . it provided the West with a political-legal wedge to judge Soviet internal affairs." He also notes that developments in global communication provided the technical means for collecting data on "internal" human rights violations. Anderson, "New World Order," 131 and 135.
The Security Council had long had available to it the opportunity to intervene with force as a consequence of the threat of international peace and security which comes with the flood of refugees across national boundaries which often accompanies systematic and widespread brutality within a state's sovereign boundaries. What is new are the technical, legal and

organizational means for intervening in the absence of or prior to such a flood of refugees. Klintworth, "'Right to Intervene,'" 253.

12. Gene M. Lyons and Michael Mastanduno, *Beyond Westphalia? International Intervention, State Sovereignty, and the Future of International Sovereignty* (Hanover: The Rockefeller Center at Dartmouth College, [1992]), 3 and 17.

13. Wright notes that the concept of state sovereignty, from an international law point of view, is identical with that of domestic jurisdiction: "*All situations with which a state may be concerned and in which its discretion is not affected by international obligations.*" Thus for the international legal scholar, sovereign independence is the freedom of a state to act without the probability of protest from any other state, with "protest" being understood as "a formal representation alleging violation of the protesting state's rights under international law." Quincy Wright, "Sovereignty and International Cooperation," in *Studies in Political Science*, Edited by J.S. Bains (New York: Asia Publishing House, 1961), 20.

14. Wright defines *absolute* sovereignty as the status of an actor with the power to do what it wants, unimpeded by law or ethics, by external restraints or internal revolts. He sees such a notion as hostile to international cooperation. So defined, most would see it as really never existing. "Sovereignty and International Cooperation," 21-22.

15. Article 2(1) of the Charter states that the UN is based on the principle of the sovereign equality of all its members. "Linguistically the expression 'sovereign equality' is not a happy one. It is not 'equality' which sustains the character of sovereignty, but the states. 'Equality as sovereign states' is obviously what is meant. This implies in the first place a recognition of the principle of sovereignty as the fundamental principle of the organization. . . ." Alf Ross, *Constitution of the United Nations: Analysis of Structure and Function* (New York: Rinehart & Company, 1950), 118.
One could argue that that fundamental principle is at odds with Article 2 (4) which prohibits states from the threat or use of force in any manner inconsistent with the UN's purposes. It has been suggested, for example, that a broad interpretation of Article 2(4) might justify UN intervention into countries possessing weapons of mass destruction, thereby serving one of the UN's highest purposes, to save future generations from the scourge of war. Klintworth, "'Right to Intervene,'" 261. Such a suggestion, of course, runs up against the Charter's unqualified provision for a state's right to its own self-defense.

16. In the post-colonial world, it is *some* members of the "third world" which have led the battle cry of non-interference in state sovereignty and the defense of Article 2(7): ". . . International acceptance of the principle of non-interference is the most important protection that historically artificial and militarily weak states have." "[S]mall states instinctively feared the consequences of any weakening of the non-intervention rule. Departure from it threatened the supremacy of the state. States demanded the right to be different and to manage their domestic economic, social and political affairs according to standards that they themselves judged appropriate." "It is not surprising that . . . so-called Third World states; who are most vulnerable to external pressures, are also most sensitive to the possible erosion of the concept of sovereignty and are most suspicious of the development of a 'right' to international intervention as a subterfuge for domination by the major powers." Klintworth, "'The Right to Intervene,'" 249. F. Gregory Gause III, "Sovereignty Statecraft and Stability in the Middle East," *Journal of International Affairs*, 45 (Winter 1992), 443. Lyons and Mastanduno, *Beyond Westphalia?*, 8. See also: Stephen D. Krasner, "Sovereignty: An Institutional Perspective," in *The Elusive State: International and Comparative Perspectives*, Edited by James A. Caporoso (Newbury Park: Sage Publications, 1989), 92-93, and Mannaraswamighal Sreeranga Rajan, *Sovereignty Over Natural Resources* (Atlantic Highlands: Humanities Press, 1978), 4.

Others, including more economically developed countries in the "third world," have objected to the emphasis on state sovereignty, especially in the economic field, fearing it might constitute a potential threat to foreign investment and ultimately prevent international economic cooperation.

Under different systemic conditions, the major powers were among those which led the battle cry: "From a legal point of view, Article 2(7) is *the quintessence of the tendency of the sovereignty dogma to resist progress*. But by the very act of investing the craving for power with the alluring draperies of this ideology they have succeeded in dazzling the small states—which have a natural desire to be recognized as 'sovereign' too—and making them accept a standpoint at variance with their own interests and the claims of law." Ross, *Constitution of the United Nations*, 129. Rajan suggests that the loss of developed countries' enthusiasm for discussing the concept of sovereignty can be linked to: (1) their views that it was less important in a globally interdependent world, and (2) their fear that it would contribute to claims of unfair treatment by natural resource (especially oil) exporting countries. *Sovereignty Over Natural Resources*, 117-21.

17. Childers makes this point well. "Until recently weak countries had four sources of protection against big-power bullying: the international law of sovereignty, the Cold War contest between the 'superpowers,' the UN and

its democratic fora; and the solidarity support of 'like-minded' governments and NGOs in the North. Of these, the Cold War has ended; the 'like-minded' seem to the South to have disappeared; and UN fora are now virtually captive to the powers' economic blackmail. Sovereignty is the last source of potential protection." Erskine Childers, "UN Mechanisms and Capacities for Intervention," in *The Challenge to Intervene: A New Role for the United Nations?*, Edited by Elizabeth G. Ferris (Uppsala: Life & Peace Institute, 1992), 49. See also: Elizabeth Ferris, "An Overview of the Issues," in *The Challenge to Intervene: A New Role for the United Nations?*, Edited by Elizabeth G. Ferris (Uppsala: Life & Peace Institute, 1992), 8.

18. This is a contentious question even in the area of human rights intervention, where the "West's" concern for human rights has often been portrayed as "cultural imperialism," that is, "We [in the West] have defined as fundamental human rights those rights which can be accorded to people in our society without posing a threat to our sociopolitical system" and now "we" are using the UN to intervene when *those* rights are being trampled." R.J. Vincent, *Human Rights and International Relations* (Cambridge: Cambridge University Press, 1986), 102. Anderson puts a slightly different gloss on the point by suggesting that moral relativism precludes intervention for human rights reasons as contrasted to moral absolutism. "New World Order," 130-31.

19. They see this as a valid criticism in spite of the fact that votes in the Security Council need four votes in addition to those of the "permanent five" to pass anything and even though the non-permanent members "often vote not only in their own right but as representatives of large clusters of countries." *Beyond Westphalia?*, 27.

20. The concept of "collective legitimization" was developed by Claude: Inis L. Claude Jr., "Collective Legitimization as a Political Function of the United Nations," *International Organization*, 20 (Summer 1966), 367-79.
Childers contends that the Security Council has been "robbed" of the confidence of "most of the UN's membership" by threats and actions of the "Northern powers" (e.g., threatening curtailment of debt relief or World Bank capital projects or enforcing tough IMF adjustment conditions if countries don't vote for them). "The Council is now regarded as a captive, where the North secures decisions by economic intimidation, abuses the peaceful-redress procedures inscribed in the Charter, and authorises actions of the North's selective choosing." "UN Mechanisms and Capacities," 46-47. Klintworth discusses one such abuse of power. "'Right to Intervene,'" 262.

Cohen provides the complementary argument to Childers'. She contends that "third world" dominance on the UN's Commission on Human Rights explains why the Commission has been so sensitive to any initiatives that could be construed as interference in a member state's internal affairs. As a consequence, the Security Council and Secretary-General have been more aggressive in human rights monitoring, often as a part of peacekeeping or overseeing elections or as part of paving the road to independence. Roberta Cohen, "UN Human Rights Bodies: An Agenda for Humanitarian Action," in *The Challenge to Intervene: A New Role for the United Nations?*, Edited by Elizabeth G. Ferris (Uppsala: Life & Peace Institute, 1992), 78.

21. This provision was inserted in the Covenant at Woodrow Wilson's insistence. "Wilson, during a journey to the U.S. after the first draft of the Covenant had observed that American public opinion was strongly opposed to League intervention in matters regarded as purely American. The questions in view were especially tariffs, immigration, citizenship, race discrimination, and the distribution of raw materials." Ross, *Constitution of the United Nations*, 119.

22. Whenever the League's Council or Assembly was accused of intervening in a member state's domestic jurisdiction, which was frequent, it was treated as a legal question. In only three instances, however, did the Permanent Court of International Justice (PCIJ) get involved. The most significant of these resulted in the PCIJ's advisory opinion relating to Tunis and Morocco (1923), namely that the acceptance by a state of a treaty obligation relating to a given subject has the effect of removing that subject from being purely domestic. Leland M. Goodrich, Edward Hambro and Anne Patricia Simons, *Charter of the United Nations: Commentary and Dissents*, Third and Revised Edition (New York: Columbia University Press, 1969), 61.

23. Rosalyn Higgins, *The Development of International Law Through the Political Organs of the United Nations* (New York: Oxford University Press, 1963), 67.

24. The change from the Covenant seems to have been a consequence of the inability of the members to decide whether the power should rest with the organization itself or the International Court of Justice, not whether it belonged to the UN or individual member states. The consequence is that members can, but need not, appeal to the relevant major organ to make the determination of whether an issue is within an individual state's domestic jurisdiction. In the case of the Security Council this allows for great power

vetoes. Ross, *Constitution of the United Nations*, 130-33. The "curious" conclusion is that: "both the United Nations as well as the Member concerned are legally entitled to interpret the question whether the reservation applies but neither is legally empowered to decide the question with binding effect on the other." Gross, *Essays*, Volume II, 1179. Gross goes on to argue that the consequence of this, legally speaking, is that members can not "block action" by the United Nations but may decline to comply with UN decisions. This, he posits, is not necessarily "fatal to the effectiveness of the United Nations," but if it is fatal, it is not due to Article 2(7), but to the absence of compulsory settlement of international disputes. In practice, UN organs act as if they have the right to make final determinations, a position seen by some as necessary to insure the Organization's effectiveness. Ibid, 1179-1180.

25. Ross, *Constitution of the United Nations*, 123. Higgins contends that the omission ". . . does not appear to have been a deliberate omission due to a belief in the inadequacy of international law, but rather due to anti-legal sentiment felt by the United States delegation and others, which were under the mistaken impression that to introduce a reference to international law would 'freeze' development." *Development of International Law*, 66.

26. Higgins, *Development of International Law*, 66.

27. *Law of the United Nations*, 773.

28. For example, one could argue that members involved in a conflict that arose from essentially domestic causes could not be required to try peaceful means of settlement prior to the outbreak of the conflict. For these reasons and others, he contends that "the wording of Article 2, paragraph 7, goes probably much further than the intention of those who drafted it." Hans Kelsen, *The Law of the United Nations: A Critical Analysis of the United Nations* (New York: Frederick A. Praeger Inc., 1951), 771-91. The change from *solely* appears to have been taken because there were assumed to be few actions that governments took domestically that didn't have "at least some external repercussions." *Report to the President on the Results of the San Francisco Conference, 26 June 1945*, as reproduced in: Louis B. Sohn, Editor, *Cases on United Nations Law* (Brooklyn, The Foundation Press, Inc., 1956), 588.

29. Ibid., 769n.

30. Ibid, 773 and 774.

31. Goodrich, Hambro and Simons, *Charter of the United Nations*, 61. Higgins goes on from there. "Moreover, it would seem that not only do the contents of this 'hard core' [of topics which always remain within the exclusive jurisdiction of the state] change in relation to the development of international relations, but even those topics which at a given time are within the domestic jurisdiction of a state may in certain circumstances still be subject to international review. . . . [A]ll that it does seem possible to say is that this 'hard core' of domestic jurisdiction topics still validly excludes direct legislative intervention by the international community in matters normally reserved to the legislation of the state: such action would certainly come within the orbit of intervention." Higgins, *Development of International Law*, 63-64. Thomson exemplifies this point by reference to the case of piracy, in which the norms of sovereign control were redefined: Janice E. Thomson, "Sovereignty in Historical Perspective: The Evolution of State Control Over Extraterritorial Violence," in *The Elusive State: International and Comparative Perspectives*, edited by James A. Caporoso (Newbury Park: Sage Publications, 1989), 250.

32. At the 7th session of the General Assembly's First Committee, however, the South African representative asserted that "discussion was one of the most effective forms of intervention of which the Assembly was capable." Quoted in: Higgins, *Development of International Law*, 70s. Earlier the South Africans had failed in their attempt to keep the issue off the General Assembly agenda. For this and related documents, see: *Repertory of Practice of the United Nations Organs*, Supplement No. 1, Volume I, Articles 1-54 of the Charter (New York: United Nations, 1958), 29-32.

33. As quoted in Sohn, *Cases and Materials*, 596. Obviously such legal rights have evolved subsequently.

34. Kelsen, *Law of the United Nations*, 772n, 773n, and 774n-775n.

35. It is worth noting that at the San Francisco conference itself, the Uruguayan delegate had stated that the UN ought not to require of its members any specific forms of government, since that would be an indirect form of intervention in the internal affairs of a state. Rajan, *Expanding Jurisdiction*, 12.

36. *N.D. White, The United Nations and the Maintenance of International Peace and Security* (Manchester: Manchester University Press, 1990), 106.

37. Such an idea, of course, could be carried to quite an extreme, and some have tried to do so. For example, India contended, during a dispute between Indonesia and the Netherlands over the former's independence, that the matter could not be one of domestic jurisdiction because it had "forced nineteen different countries in Asia and the Pacific to meet at very short notice and to pass a unanimous resolution indicating the gravity of the situation." Higgins, *Development of International Law*, 79 and 80.

38. White, *United Nations*, 106-107.

39. Ibid. This was evident by the time of the UN's discussion of Southern Rhodesia. It was, of course, a change from the earliest days when the French were able to prevail—using domestic jurisdiction arguments and others—on the question of Algeria's right to self-determination. Higgins, *Development of International Law*, 95-97 and 102-106.

40. White, *United Nations*, 107. The relevant passages for this discussion are reproduced in Sohn, *Cases and Materials*, 670-90. The Soviet position was that the UN was interfering in the domestic affairs of the Soviet Union; Soviet women preferred not to join their husbands in countries which were notoriously anti-Soviet.

41. Rajan, *Expanding Jurisdiction*, 90-91.

42. White, *United Nations*, 107-108.

43. Schachter's discussion of this point in regard to the Security Council bears quoting because it puts the domestic jurisdiction limitation in its proper perspective. "Some of the worst examples of mass killing (such as Burundi, Cambodia, and Ethiopia) have not brought armed humanitarian intervention by international bodies or concerned states. . . . No doubt genocide could be a threat to peace in that it might precipitate protective armed action by concerned states, resulting in war. That this has rarely occurred has sometimes been attributed to respect for the sovereignty of the culpable government, but the more realistic reason is that the material costs, especially in human lives, of an intervention are not perceived as justified by the national interests of other states." "Sovereignty and Threats to Peace," 25, 35 and 36. Henrikson seems to agree with Schachter's observations, but wants things to change: "There should be no automatic shielding of

malfeasance under national 'sovereignty' any longer." Alan K. Henrikson, "How Can the Vision of a 'New World Order' be Realized?" *The Fletcher Forum of World Affairs*, 16 (Winter 1992), 63.

44. See, e.g., Brian Urquhart, *A Life in Peace and War* (New York: Harper & Row, Publishers, 1987), chapters 12 and 16.

Liu makes the interesting observation that "the Security Council can, in theory, pressure the involved parties to accept a UN peacekeeping operation and cooperate with it by threatening to take enforcement measures under Chapter VII of the Charter if they do not comply." This is portrayed as potentially a quite powerful means of influence if the Security Council is capable of enforcement measures, the chances for which are considerably greater in the post-Cold War period. F.T. Liu, *United Nations Peacekeeping and the Non-Use of Force*, International Peace Academy Occasional Paper Series (Boulder: Lynne Rienner Publishers, Inc., 1992), 39. His observation contrasts with, updates or at least supplements Chee's more traditional perspective that the UN has been reluctant to get involved in domestic civil wars because it *needs an invitation.* Chee points to the UN, initially at least, deferring to the Conference on Security and Cooperation in Europe (CSCE) in the case of the former state Yugoslavia, and to the Economic Community of West African States (ECOWAS) in the case of Liberia in 1990. Chan Heng Chee, "The United Nations: From Peace-keeping to Peace-Making?," in *New Dimensions in International Security*, Part 1 of Adelphi Paper #265 (London: The International Institute for Strategic Studies, 1992), 39-40.

45. "Should the Security Council consider that measures [not involving the use of armed forces] provided for in Article 41 would be inadequate or have proved to be inadequate, it may take such action by air, sea, or land forces as may be necessary to maintain or restore international peace and security. Such action may include demonstrations, blockades, and other operations by air, sea, or land forces of Members of the United Nations."

46. Interestingly, the *travaux préparatoires* indicate that the restriction of the exception to "enforcement measures" was deliberate. Still international legal scholars contend that there are "good grounds for arguing that the other measures contemplated under Chapter VII could not be such as to constitute intervention in matters essentially within the domestic jurisdiction of any state." Higgins, *Development of International Law*, 87.

47. There were also those who questioned whether Article 2(7) was at all relevant to the Congo crisis, given that the UN was in the Congo at that government's request in the first place. The fact that it was there at the request of the Congolese government seemed a not very serious legal

argument, at least not serious to objective legal scholars analyzing it. As Higgins argued, the fact that the UN was invited into the Congo "does not mean . . . that the sovereign right of domestic jurisdiction can be safely—or legally—ignored by the United Nations at will. Beyond [the] rights of actions expressly or by reasonable implication designated to it for the fulfillment of its mandate, ONUC [UN troops in the Congo] remains bound by the provisions of Article 2(7)." *Development of International Law*, 107.

48. This happened, for example, in terms of a request from the Rumanian government. *New York Times* (January 24, 1990), A12, col. 5.

49. See, e.g., Thomas M. Franck, "United Nations Based Prospects for a New Global Order; Seizing the Moment: Creative and Incremental Thinking about Global Systemic Opportunity," *New York University Journal of International Law and Politics*, 22 (Summer 1990), 634n-635n.

50. For example in the Namibian case, the agreement to conduct election monitoring was part of the UN plan for Namibian independence accepted by the Security Council on September 29, 1979 and worked out with South Africa over the following decade. "Namibia: A Nation is Born," *Objective Justice*, 22 (June 1990), 1. The Nicaraguan observers flowed directly out of the Guatemalan agreement (also known as Esquipulas II), signed on August 7, 1989. "The Situation in Central America: Threats to International Peace and Security and Peace Initiatives," Note by the Secretary-General, A/44/642.

51. "Haiti Holds Free, Democratic Election with UN Help," *UN Chronicle* (March 1991), 62.

52. Mexico's leadership role in its concern with interference in countries' internal affairs is long-standing. During the General Assembly's 1946 debate on South Africa's treatment of Indians, the Mexican delegate de la Colina referred to his country as "being a champion of the principle of non-intervention." Sohn, *Cases and Materials*, 602.

53. "U.N. Mission Dispatched to Haiti," *UN Chronicle* (September 1990), 10.

54. On the opposition, led by Mexico, Colombia, Cuba and Yemen, see: Paul Lewis, "Haiti Wants U.N. to Monitor Vote," *New York Times* (July 22, 1990), A10, column 6.

Evidence, more generally, on the split within the General Assembly on this issue can be found in comparing General Assembly Resolution 45/150 ("Enhancing the Effectiveness of the Principle of Periodic and Genuine Elections") with General Assembly Resolution 45/151 ("Respect for the Principles of National Sovereignty and Non-interference in the Internal Affairs of States in their Electoral Processes"). Both were passed on December 18, 1989. A/RES/45/150 and A/RES/45/151.

55. United Nations. General Assembly. A/45/PV.29, 64-65. See also the letter dated 17 July 1990 from the Permanent Representatives of the Bahamas, Colombia and Haiti to the United Nations addressed to the President of the General Assembly. A/44/965/Addendum.1, 1.

56. In addition to Mexico's frequent, hardly veiled allusions to post U.S. intervention in Latin America, that country's opposition may be part of a bargaining strategy. Such seems implicit, at least, in Franck's contention that the opposition from Mexico and other "third world" countries ". . . to systemic reform seems to be gaining ground among the states of the Third World, suggesting the need to make the Third World's economic agenda a part of any conference on systemic reform." Franck, "United Nations," 613.

Mexico's position was that of one particular "third world" country. The "third world" was hardly united on this question.

57. Such a development would seemingly be in line with the wishes of those scholars—like Lapidoth—who believe that concepts should be related ". . . to the civilization prevailing at a certain period, and a drastic change in the political environment [such as the collapse of the chief ideological challenge to classical liberalism] may entail a new meaning or nuance to an old concept." Ruth Lapidoth, "Sovereignty in Transition," *Journal of International Affairs*, 45 (Winter 1992), 326. For a very different rationale, but one which ends up at a similar point, see: Sohail H. Hashmi, "Is There an Islamic Ethic of Humanitarian Intervention?," *Ethics & International Affairs*, 7 (1993), 55-73.

58. Kim R. Holmes, "New World Disorder: A Critique of the United Nations," *Journal of International Affairs*, 46 (Winter 1993), 327.

59. Franck, "United Nations," 637.

60. Ibid., 637-38 and 639.

61. United Nations. General Assembly. Fifth Committee. "Provisional Verbatim Record of the 26th Meeting." October 9, 1990. A/45/PV.26.

62. See "Letter Dated 5 October 1990 From the President of the Security Council Addressed to the Secretary-General," United Nations, Security Council, S/21847. See also the letter from the Haitian government, dated 17 September 1990 (S/21846 and Appendix II of A/44/973) and the letter from the Secretary-General to the President of the Security Council dated 7 September 1990, S/21845.

63. Lewis, "Haiti Wants U.N.," A10, col. 6.

64. Of course previous examples exist in which the U.S., in the context of the UN, led the fight to break down the barriers of national sovereignty. Among the most notable in this regard relates to the so-called New International Communications Order and specifically the U.S. opposition to limits on the rights of direct television broadcasting, including the right of states to "prior consent." In this instance, which is well described by Nordenstreng and Schiller, the U.S. stood alone . . . against a united "third world," UNESCO secretariat and even its traditional "first world" allies. Kaarle Nordenstreng and Herbert I. Schiller, "Introduction to Part 2," in *National Sovereignty and International Communication*, edited by Kaarle Nordenstreng and Herbert I. Schiller (Norwood: Ablex Publishing Corporation, 1979), 115-118.

65. Concern had earlier been expressed by a number of "third world" countries during the UN Security Council's consideration of extending its concerns to cover drug trafficking. Lewis, "Haiti Wants U.N.," *New York Times* (July 22, 1990), A10, col. 6.

66. "United Nations," 628.

67. "Sovereignty and Threats to Peace," 26.

68. Bruce Russett, "A Post-Thucydides, Post-Cold War World," *Mediterranean Quarterly: A Journal of Global Issues*, 4 (Winter 1993), 52. Such a policy would be a clear divergence from the past as well summarized by Eide. "To a large extent, the United Nations has accepted the establishment of political units as they stand, irrespective of the way in which they came into being, be it by imperial expansion or by a deliberate social contract among the ancestors of those who live in the country. The United Nations has been active in the field of decolonization but has

otherwise left rather open the issue of whether the current political units called states are the appropriate frameworks for the exercise of sovereignty by the people concerned." Asbjørn Eide, "National Sovereignty and International Efforts to Realize Human Rights," in *Human Rights in Perspective: A Global Assessment*, edited by Asbjørn Eide and Brent Hagtvet (Oxford: Basil Blackwell, Ltd., 1992), 28.

69. Including two votes taken on the same day (December 18, 1990), in the UN General Assembly. The first, passed 128-8-9, asserted that "[p]eriodic and genuine elections are a necessary and indispensable element of sustained efforts to protect the rights and interests of the governed." The second, passed 118-29-11, called for "[r]espect for principles of national sovereignty and non-interference in the international affairs of states in their electoral processes." Marks concludes that the UN's increased call for involvement in elections "gives rise to some controversy." Marks, *United Nations and Human Rights*, 5.

70. See especially Judge Shahabudden's separate opinion in the ICJ case relating to Libya's request for provisional measures against the United States and United Kingdom for those countries' participation in the Security Council's actions against Libya.

71. See also: Oscar Schachter, "United Nations Law in the Gulf Conflict," *The American Journal of International Law*, 85 (July 1991), 452-73.

72. Van Boven draws a useful distinction between the long-standing (and in his view largely non-interventionist) practice of supervisory activities (where countries are made accountable for reports on infringements) and monitoring (which he portrays as clearly interventionist, and thus requiring a much higher threshold for actualization). Theo Van Boven, Book Review of *Humanitarian Norms and Customary International Law*, *The American Journal of International Law*, 85 (January 1991), 213.

73. See, for example, Lyons and Mastanduno, *Beyond Westphalia?*, 19-20. For an interesting compilation of documents related to this point see: Fred Tanner, Editor, *From Versailles to Baghdad: Post-War Armament Control of Defeated States*, UNIDIR/92/70 (New York: United Nations, 1992).

74. "Drawing on the lessons of the war and its wake, some in the West heralded the demise of sovereignty: French Humanitarian Affairs Minister Kouchner coined the 'droit d'ingerence.'" Michael Stopford, "The Limits of

International Action: Solidarity and Sovereignty," Address Given at the American University Conference, "Human Rights for the 21st Century: Perspectives from the Global South," April 19 1993, 7-8. But also note that there was ambivalence in some quarters of "the North." Indeed, a former editor of the *Times of London* prophesied that if the UN continued in this vein ". . . the outcome will be a spasmodic adventurism born of cynicism out of racism. It will thoroughly discredit the UN." As quoted in Ibid., 9.

75. Clovis Maksoud described the Security's Council's recent actions as "symptomatic of the United Nations' inherent tendency to fluctuate between immobility and excessive action." As recounted in Peter J. Fromuth, "The Making of a Security Community: The United Nations After the Cold War," *Journal of International Affairs*, 46 (Winter 1993), 355.

76. In this regard, Urquhart's sensible suggestion seems too limited a perspective on the lessons learned from the Gulf War. Thinking of the clarity of Iraq's aggression and the unprecedented Great Power consensus in the Security Council he contended that: "It would be unwise to base thinking about the future of international security—or indeed the United Nations—too much on the Gulf experience." Brian Urquhart, "The United Nations: From Peace-keeping to a Collective System," in *New Directions in International Security*, part 1 of Adelphi Paper #265 (London: The International Institute for Strategic Studies, 1992), 19. While that is certainly true, it overlooks the Gulf's impacts on perceptions of so-called third world countries and, as this chapter tries to suggest, the UN itself.

77. Some of this posturing was explained in terms of his desire to be an acceptable mediator. Ibid., 160.

78. Ibid., 145 and 268.

79. Ernst B. Haas, "Collective Conflict Management: Evidence for a New World Order?," in *Collective Security in a Changing World*, edited by Thomas G. Weiss (Boulder: Lynne Rienner Publishers, 1993), 80-81.

80. Quoted in Richard N. Gardner, "International Law and the Use of Force," in *New Dimensions in_International Security*, Part II of Adelphi Paper #266 (London: The International Institute for Strategic Studies, 1992), 71.

81. Haas, "Collective Conflict Management," 80.

82. Gardner, "International Law and the Use of Force," 71.

83. Jarat Chopra, "The Obsolescence of *Intervention* Under International Law," in *Sovereignty and the Right to Intervene* (Miami: University of Florida Press, forthcoming), 2-3.

84. See, for example: Tony P. Hall, "The Humanitarian Agenda in the New World Order," *Mediterranean Quarterly*, 3 (Fall 1992), 6.

85. Larry Minear and Thomas G. Weiss, "Groping and Coping in the Gulf Crisis: Discerning the Shape of a New Humanitarian Order," *World Policy Journal*, 9 (Fall/Winter 1992), 762-63.

86. Jarat Chopra and Thomas G. Weiss, "Sovereignty Is No Longer Sacrosanct: Codifying Humanitarian Intervention," *Ethics and International Affairs*, 6 (1992), 95.

87. In a similar vein, President Sommargua of the International Committee of the Red Cross (ICRC) has been reported to have argued that armed intervention jeopardizes the neutrality essential for the delivery of humanitarian relief: "it becomes part of the problem, it starts taking sides." Stopford, "Limits of International Action," 8.

88. Haas, "Collective Conflict Management," 80-81.

89. A recent article in *The Pioneer*, a newspaper from New Delhi, maintained that "there is no legal sanction for the enforcement of humanitarian aid. . . ." He suggested that the Security Council was being asked to "lend a cloak of legality to blatant interference in Iraq's internal affairs" and suggested instead that the non-aligned movement should propose procedures, in the UN General Assembly, "to regulate the proper delivery of humanitarian aid." Similarly, the Zimbabwe Ambassador on the Security Council was quoted on CNN as complaining that the definition of a "threat to international peace and security" was anything that the Security Council decided it to be. As reported by: Stopford, "Limits of International Action," 8. See also, for example, Khalifa's and Roakoun's comments: "Summary Record of the 10th Meeting of the Sub-Commission on Prevention of Discrimination and Protection of Minorities of the Commission on Human Rights," 43rd Session (August 13, 1991), E/CN/4/Sub.2/1991/SR.10, 6. "Summary Record of the 3rd Meeting of the 48th Session of the Commission on Human Rights" (February 19, 1992), E/CN4/1992/SR.33, 9.

90. As Greenwood notes, the threat to neighboring countries, never great, was "arguably receding by the time Resolution 794 was adopted." "Is There a Right to Humanitarian Intervention?," 40.

91. Haas, "Collective Conflict Management," 81-82.

92. Robert H. Jackson, *Quasi-States: Sovereignty, International Relations, and the Third World* (Cambridge: Cambridge University Press, 1990).

93. This would be keeping with the wishes of scholars like Henrikson who call for an articulate, theoretical justification and clear-cut guidelines for collective intervention. "How Can the Vision," 63.

94. Others have expressed similar concerns. See, for example: Muzaffar, "Some Observations on UN Intervention," 125; Brian Urquhart, "The United Nations: From Peace-keeping to a Collective System" in *New Directions in International Security*, part 1 of Adelphi Paper #265 (London: The International Institute for Strategic Studies, 1992), 26; and Abdullahi Anhmed Na'im, "Third World Perspectives" in *The Challenge to Intervene: A New Role for the United Nations?*, edited by Elizabeth G. Ferris (Uppsala: Life & Peace Institute, 1992), 143-44. See also footnotes 15-19 above.

95. This was evident in General Assembly debates in December of 1991. Minear and Weiss, "Groping and Coping," 774.